le Evelyn
Christmas 1996

Local History

Local History

A HANDBOOK FOR BEGINNERS

Philip Riden

B.T. Batsford Ltd
London

© Philip Riden 1983
First published 1983
Reprinted 1988
Reprinted with revisions 1989

Typeset by Deltatype, Ellesmere Port, South Wirral
and printed in Great Britain by
Biddles Ltd
Guildford Surrey

for the publishers
B.T. Batsford Ltd
4 Fitzhardinge Street
London W1H 0AH

British Library Cataloguing in Publication Data

Riden, Philip
  Local history.
  1. Great Britain—History, Local
  I. Title
  941   DA34

ISBN 0–7134–3870–3
ISBN 0–7134–3871–1 Pbk

CONTENTS

PREFACE

This book is based broadly on lectures which I have given to adult classes and other groups in various places since 1975. My principal debt is therefore to the large numbers of students who have already heard most of what is written here and in many cases made helpful comments or criticisms or suggested new ideas to me. I am particularly grateful to the Director of Extra-Mural Studies at University College, Cardiff, where I have taught since 1977 and had most opportunity to develop the teaching of local history to adult students and to draw on the resources of a university to promote the amateur study of local history generally. I also owe a debt to Professor W. E. Minchinton of the University of Exeter, in whose department I had the (fairly rare) opportunity to teach local history to undergraduate economic historians. Numerous colleagues in several different parts of the country have, knowingly or unknowingly, put ideas into my head which have ended up here, especially fellow members of the Association of Local History Tutors. At University College members of the Department of the History of Wales have been consistently generous in initiating me into the mysteries of their field; I have also benefited from discussions with Matthew Griffiths, Clive Knowles and Brian James, of whom the last named read the whole of the book in draft. That unenviable task was also cheerfully and helpfully undertaken by Dudley Fowkes, for many years a mainstay of local history in my home county of Derbyshire, who considerably improved Chapters 3 and 4. Derek Jones of Chesterfield and Roy Chamberlain of University College, Cardiff, produced the final versions of most of the illustrations.

For permission to reproduce Figure 6 I am indebted to the Glamorgan Archive Service, the owner of the original photograph (D/D X66/2), and for permission to reproduce Figure 10 the Derbyshire Centre for Geography and Environmental Studies at Matlock College of Higher Education. Figures 3 and 4 are reproduced by courtesy of the National Library of Wales; Figures 1 and 2 by courtesy of the Derbyshire Archaeological Society (publishers of a complete facsimile of the map in question); and Figures 7, 8 and 9 by courtesy of the Derbyshire County Librarian. The illustration used on the cover of the book is reproduced by courtesy of the Librarian, University College, Cardiff.

As I explain in Chapter 1, local history textbooks have been appearing in roughly their present form since 1879 (the last occasion, incidentally, when a book of this kind, based heavily on Derbyshire experience, was published); the expansive 1960s and 1970s, when the subject flourished mightily in all branches of education, saw a particular efflorescence of books for beginners and others. My aim in writing this modest addition to the list is basically two-fold: to provide a simpler (but still reliable) introduction to the subject than W. B. Stephens's standard textbook, which is probably used mainly by undergraduates and lecturers rather than amateur enthusiasts; and to give advice, aimed especially at beginners starting an extra-mural course or just generally interested, that is up-to-date and realistic. With the reduction in the growth of public spending on education, libraries, record offices and the like in recent years, some of the suggestions made in books only five or ten years ago now sound very optimistic. Mine is I hope a book for the straitened eighties and it is on this basis that I should like it to be judged.

Philip Riden
Cardiff, February 1983

Chapter One
LOCAL HISTORY TODAY

The aim of this book is to provide a simple introduction to the study of local history. It is intended mainly for part-time amateur enthusiasts with no previous experience of historical research who are keen to discover something of the past around them. Such people have probably never been as numerous as they are today, as is evident from the support for local history groups up and down the country, the popularity of evening classes, and (somewhat to the embarrassment of their staffs) the demand for the services of county record offices and the local studies departments of public libraries. This vigorous amateur interest is paralleled by the popularity of the subject in universities, especially for higher degree dissertations, and in polytechnics and colleges.

This phenomenon has inevitably brought with it an upsurge in publication, ranging from substantial academic monographs through the mass of books and pamphlets published by individual local historians or societies, to the ephemeral newsletters of such groups, as well as the more scholarly annual volumes of the older county antiquarian societies. Among the welter of recent books are several which provide instruction in how to study local history. The pioneer of this sort of book was W. G. Hoskins, who from the late 1940s was popularising the 'Leicester School' of local history in articles and broadcasts. Others at work in the same period produced not merely many excellent examples of the 'new local history' of communities in which they were interested, but also 'how to do it' books or occasionally 'why do it'. The last ten years have seen more textbooks, while some of the most popular aspects of amateur local history—industrial archaeology, family history and 'how to trace the history of your house'—have substantial literatures of their own. Amid all this work, good, bad and indifferent, one book stands out, and indeed has become a quarry of information for its rivals. This is W. B. Stephens's *Sources for English Local History*, now in its third, carefully revised edition, which provides an authoritative guide to the primary and secondary, printed and unprinted, sources for those aspects of local history most studied in universities and colleges, and to some extent by amateurs. It is unlikely that Stephens will be superseded for at least a generation, as long as it is kept up-to-date, and imitation seems unnecessary.

The present book has most emphatically not been written to rival Stephens, or even to simplify it for wider consumption. It has been written in the belief that there is scope for a short handbook on 'how to get started', not how to write the definitive community history or a higher degree thesis. I have written it against a background of my own interest in local history—largely untutored—since my early teens; ten years' experience of teaching adult classes in the subject (mostly as full-time tutor for a university extramural department with a large local history programme); and wide contact with other local historians, librarians and archivists in several different parts of the country. Above all, the book has been written with extramural students in mind, and for the large number of people interested in local history, often actively involved in research, who do not support extramural classes but who tend to ask the same questions. While there have been many forces at work to make local history as popular as it is today, arguably it has been adult education which has contributed most. Extramural tutors probably meet more amateur local historians than any other group concerned with the subject, and know the sort of things amateurs, especially beginners, want to know. Extramural students taking an 'advanced' course in local history, for a certificate or diploma, can be recommended Professor Stephens's book, as can students in colleges writing undergraduate dissertations. Those with a more casual interest, especially if they are coming to the subject for the first time, may well find an academic monograph offputting. It is for them that this book has been written.

In the chapters that follow the reader will find a clear, up-to-date guide to basic sources for local history, plus hints as to where to find out more. Each chapter has a bibliography. Apart from the larger textbooks, there is now an enormous literature on particular sources or research topics, which, together with the more general references, should lead the amateur researcher beyond the fairly modest limits of this book. What this book should do, however, is provide a sound grounding in what local history is about, how it is studied, and how any interested person can discover more about the past around them.

Most books on sources for local history progress from an introductory chapter on why the book is better than any of its rivals to taking each aspect of the subject in turn and explaining how to find out about it. Thus one has chapters on local government, education, religion, transport and so on. This is fine, and in very detailed books probably the only way to organise a mass of information. But it is not, as any extramural tutor, archivist or librarian will know, how most amateurs work. The beginner in local history may well be interested in only one aspect of his community, or in some theme not amenable to study within a parish (e.g. industrial archaeology or family history). If he is generally interested in the history of his town or village he will soon be overwhelmed by what is available and narrow down his interest to one topic—say, the development of communications, or the community as viewed through the enumerators' books of a single census. The other possibility is that his interest will widen out from a very narrow starting-point—the history of his own house or family, or the history of a single industrial enterprise.

However the amateur enthusiast starts, one thing is certain. He will not, as the arrangement of some of the weightier textbooks suggests he should, take a topic (say transport in a local community) and start working through all the secondary literature (which in this case is huge, and for which he will need the resources of a big city library, if not a university) listed in the textbooks. Even more certainly, he will not work systematically through the primary sources for his chosen subject, wherever they may be (for transport history much material is held in London in places which the amateur living in the provinces can usually only visit occasionally). He will instead go to his local library, look at what is available in the reference department on transport history, and then go to the local studies section to see what they have on the immediate locality. His next step will be to go to the county record office, in the hope of finding more from local archive material. Only after working in this way for some time will most amateurs go to the Public Record Office or one of the other central repositories, or follow up obscure printed references in a copyright library or a major academic or public library. Beginners want to be told how they can make worthwhile discoveries quickly from what is available to hand, not given a long list of widely scattered archival sources or a vast bibliography of printed material, much of which can only be found in a few libraries.

Similarly, most amateur local historians do not need the thoroughness of some of the published work on particular records. For example, while almost all local historians use maps, few use quarter sessions records, which feature in most of the textbooks but are some of the least produced documents in county record offices. Similarly, with two conspicuous exceptions (bishops' transcripts of parish registers and probate records), the non-parochial records of the Church of England are also, despite the existence of a thorough guide, little used except by academic researchers. This book does not aim to list every possible source for a particular topic, nor does it describe everything to be found in a county record office. It concentrates on subjects which amateurs tend to be interested in, and material available in local libraries and record offices which they can use without encountering great technical problems.

Another consideration is that not all parts of England and Wales offer the same scope for local history. (As in all books of this kind, Scotland is omitted, since its administrative and judicial history have created a separate system of records which cannot easily be dealt with alongside sources for England and Wales.) Most of the archival material used by local historians is the product of an administrative process, mainly at local level, and the English counties have had the same administrative arrangements since the middle ages. Wales was shired by Henry VIII and since then the Welsh counties have been subject to the same legislation (with a few exceptions) as those in England. Similarly, the local administrative history of the Church of England (including until 1920 four Welsh dioceses) has been uniform for a very long time. What is sometimes not made clear is that different parts of the country have vastly dissimilar histories of archive *preservation*, even if archive *creation* originally took a similar form everywhere. In general, the Home Counties and those of southern England have the best preserved records, those of the north and west, and even more the Welsh counties, the least. Discoveries of this kind can be disappointing to a beginner, who has identified what should be available from a textbook and seeks out such material in a local record office. For example, the everyday lives of yeoman farmers in Tudor Devon cannot, despite what the textbooks may say, be recreated from that county's share of the thousands of probate inventories that survive in every county record office: most of the Exeter probate records were destroyed during the last war. This problem is most acute in Wales, where whole tracts of early modern material simply do not survive, and where local history is frankly often a frustrating experience before about 1750. I have tried to be more realistic than some other writers whose experience seems to be drawn only from a richly endowed Home Counties record office.

A similar problem often exists with the material in county record offices that has been deposited privately. It is not always made clear that the existence of a manor does not necessarily mean that the record office will have court rolls from 1300 to 1925, while most textbooks notoriously exaggerate the survival of business records (businessmen have always been far too busy to keep proper records, or to be interested in preserving them; some industries, e.g. coal, have had a positive interest in destroying archives). Similarly, the vagaries of landownership have not always produced the tons of estate material which most local record offices have for certain major families. A great deal may have been burnt when a mansion was pulled down in 1920, or when it was requisitioned by the army in 1939. Likewise, despite the impression given in some quarters, solicitors earn a living by acting for clients, not devoting time and space to the preservation of old papers until the record office seeks to take them on deposit. Some old established firms never make deposits, some have nothing to deposit because it was all destroyed in a fire two years ago.

These observations may bring comfort to archivists worn down by explaining that their holdings do not correspond in every particular with what it says in a general guide; they may seem depressing to the intending local historian. He should not worry unduly: he will almost certainly be able to discover something about the topic he is interested in. But common sense should tell him that some county councils are more generous than others in how many staff they provide for their record office, or how large a searchroom or strongroom. Some offices have been in existence for much longer than others; not only have they had more time to collect records but, equally as important, they have had longer to list and index them. Exactly the same is true of local studies libraries, which vary greatly in the richness of their holdings and the service they offer the public.

Although the present approach to local history owes much to the work of early post-war enthusiasts such as W. G. Hoskins, as developed and refined by many people over the last generation, the subject is very much older. Hoskins and others grew up during a particularly sterile period in English local history—the inter-war years—in which there was little innovation and the institutions which had served local history before the first war were in decline, with nothing to replace them. The new teaching and research at Leicester and elsewhere took local history out of the doldrums and sent it in exciting new directions. But looking further back there was another golden age, between about 1870 and 1914. And so it goes on, with periods of vitality interspersed with periods of quiescence or stagnation, back to the beginning of antiquarianism, which is one small facet of the reception of the Renaissance in England in the second half of the sixteenth century. Today's local historians owe more than they are sometimes willing to admit to the long history of their own subject, especially the buoyant periods of that history. In the first place, there is a legacy of local topographical writing—the secondary published sources with which virtually all research begins—which can best be understood in the context of the development of the subject. Coupled with this is an important archival legacy of 'antiquarian papers', compiled by past local historians, containing extracts from records, notes on church monuments, and sometimes descriptions of field monuments. This material is often ignored by present-day local historians, but it is important as part of the 'history of local history' (more broadly, the history of ideas) and can often be a valuable source. A third reason why local historians should know something about the history of their subject is that much of the institutional framework within which local history is organised, for both part-time enthusiasts and academics, is best explained historically. Why, for example, should a body with the eminently reasonable name of 'British Association for Local History' have been founded only in 1982?

While the study of History in the widest sense is one of the oldest pursuits of civilisation, the same is not true of what we now know as local history. Looking simply at England, it is fair to say that most medieval people were not interested in topography. Contemporary chronicles of course mention localities associated with political or military events, and some of the minor chronicles form a source for the local history of the places in which they were written. But people did not travel up and down the country for pleasure, nor, for the most part, did they draw maps and plans. With very few exceptions medieval historians did not search archives for local source material, or write descriptions of where they lived.

The influence of the new learning in Elizabethan England led to the complete rewriting of English political history for the first time since the twelfth century; men also became interested in local history. This interest took two main directions. On the one hand were those antiquaries, most often lawyers or men who had spent some time at an Inn of Court, who searched the archives of central government for references to their own county, starting with Domesday Book (1086), the oldest public record which has been continuously in official custody, and proceeding through later material, all of it heavily biased towards the history of landowner-ship and the descent of manors. Parallel with this interest arose a fascination for genealogy which, with ups and downs, has lasted to the present. The great promoters of sixteenth-century family history were the heralds, who in the course of their perambulations around the country (the Visitations) noted not merely the pedigrees of landed families but also heraldic glass in church and manor-house windows and monuments in churches with heraldic decoration. As in later ages, the professional heralds were imitated by amateur enthusiasts. Thus, at the same time as families in the peerage were beginning to send their sons on the 'Grand Tour' of southern Europe to view the newly rediscovered splendours of Greece and Rome, the gentry, with their more modest but nonetheless broadening horizons, were looking for the first time at their 'country', meaning the county in which they had their estate, in which they were a justice of the peace, and which was the focus of their political, economic and social life.

By the 1570s this interest in genealogy and topography was beginning to bear fruit in published work. The earliest 'county history' is usually reckoned to be William Lambarde's *Kent* (1576), written by a lawyer and, not surprisingly, devoted to one of the Home Counties. Before the end of the century works had been published for several other counties and much more had been collected but not published. The first half of the seventeenth century saw a development of this literature until in 1656 the herald and future Garter King of Arms William Dugdale published his *Warwickshire*. This marked the high point of pre-Restoration local history and was imitated a good deal after 1660, for example in Robert Thoroton's *Nottinghamshire* of 1677.

Dugdale's *Warwickshire*, in its format and content, epitomises the first century of English antiquarianism. In the first place it was the work of a gentleman. The landed gentry or gentry-lawyers practically monopolised this era of antiquarian writing: the antiquary-cleric of eighteenth-century caricatures belongs to a later period. Secondly, it was divided into two parts of unequal length. The book began with a general description of its chosen county, its size, supposed population, administrative geography, markets and fairs, rivers and hills, and 'political history' from the Anglo-Saxon heptarchy to the present. Having summarised the essential features of the county as a whole, the author proceeded to describe each place within it, either listing the parishes in alphabetical order or, more likely, arranging them by 'Hundred', the ancient subdivision of a county in southern England, known in the East Midlands and North as a 'Wapentake'. The account of each parish would be taken up very largely by two topics: the manor and its owners since 1086 and the church and its contents, especially monuments. The more ambitious county history sometimes introduced other material, either in the 'general section' or under the appropriate parish: discoveries of prehistoric or Roman antiquities, charitable benefactions, interesting natural phenomena. The more legally-minded the author, the more emphasis there would be on manorial history; if, alternatively, he was more interested in heraldry, church monuments and topography, there would be a bias in that direction. Overall, however, the scope of the early county history was very limited and for this reason has little appeal to modern local historians.

The first generation of county histories is significant partly as a reflection of educated men's views of their locality in the sixteenth and seventeenth centuries: their view of the county as the natural unit about which to write, even though they did not normally use county records; their emphasis on the manor and manorial tenures, sometimes to the exclusion of lesser landowning families in a parish; and their more or less careful recording of church monuments, with domestic architecture, including even manor houses, often wholly ignored. Secondly, the books are important because they determined the mould in which local history would be written down to 1914 and even beyond: the division of the county into parishes and manors; the division of the history into 'general' and 'parochial' sections. But they are also still useful today, especially the more ambitious seventeenth-century compilations. Despite their old-fashioned arrangement and content, the county histories often provide the most thorough account of the history of a manor and of the families that owned it. There is far more to village history today than the descent of the manor, but in many parts of the country the manor remained an important local institution until the nineteenth century, and to know who was the main landowner in a parish is the obvious starting-point in any search for manorial or estate records.

Similarly, the description of the church may seem irrelevant, but the building could have been entirely altered by the Victorians, leaving a seventeenth-century account as the only guide to what it looked like when the men and women listed in the first parish register were baptised, married and buried there. For a local historian working on nineteenth-century brickmaking there will not be much in the traditional county history, but someone interested in the community as a whole should not deride the stately volumes in which so many of these histories were published, even if their authors' views of the local community were very different from ours.

By the middle of the eighteenth century, histories had appeared for most English counties. The period 1660–1730 was one of great scholarship in English history and this was reflected in local topography, as some of the 'Friends of Clio' who formed the readership for the new history tried their hand at writing. The half-century after 1730 was less productive but between about 1780 and 1830 there was a new upsurge of interest, partly on familiar lines, but in other ways breaking new ground. Several of the older histories were re-issued, usually with 'Additions' claiming to bring them up to date: thus Thoroton's *Nottinghamshire* re-appeared in three volumes instead of one in 1790. Counties of which no previous account had been published were described for the first time but still in an entirely traditional manner: Theophilus Jones's *Brecknockshire* (1805–9) is a remarkable example of this in a poor, thinly populated Welsh county. Leicestershire, for which William Burton provided a brief history as early as 1622, practically sank under the endeavours of the antiquarian publisher John Nichols.

What was new in English antiquarianism during the first generation of its 'Romantic' phase was the emergence of the travel account as a distinct branch of topographical writing. There are a few well known earlier travel diaries, such as those of Celia Fiennes or Daniel Defoe, but the great growth of such literature dates from after 1750, and especially the half-century before the coming of the railway virtually killed the genre. Some of these books are purely descriptive; some, such as Arthur Young's tours, have a specialist interest in improvements in farming. Others, such as William Bray's *Sketch of a Tour into Derbyshire and Yorkshire* (1782), are solidly antiquarian and provide, often with numerous engraved plates, descriptions not merely of churches but also of medieval domestic buildings, archaeological discoveries and much else. Works of this kind are invariably worth checking in case the tourist mentions the place you are interested in, and early tours may provide the first reference anywhere to archaeological features then being uncovered. Tour literature must be treated with some caution, however: some accounts are fictitious and merely describe journeys around their author's library of similar works; rather more are based on genuine tours but reiterate what previous visitors said about much-visited places (e.g. Bath or the Wonders of the Peak), adding nothing new.

The tour diary spawned a more local literature of guidebooks about particular places or guides to country houses, then being increasingly visited by the new tourists; it also had some influence on the writing of county history. More topographical description and more field archaeology crept in alongside the pedigrees and arms; ruins of religious houses and castles were described as well as the church. The first phase in the history of archaeology as a separate discipline also belongs to this period and is reflected not only in tours and county histories but in new journals, of which *Archaeologia*, published by the Society of Antiquaries of London, was the most important. The beginning of the nineteenth century saw a spate of short-lived journals rivalling both *Archaeologia* and the *Gentleman's Magazine* as outlets for antiquarian writing, most of which were not, like their successors later in the century, produced by societies but by the same commercial publishers who were producing the county histories, tour books and collections of prints of the same period.

Finally, it is worth mentioning—especially for readers in counties lying alphabetically between Bedfordshire and Devonshire—the most ambitious county history scheme of these years, *Magna Britannia*, an attempt to produce uniform histories of every English county. Daniel and Samuel Lysons, one a record keeper in the Tower of London, the other a Cotswold parson, were not the first to conceive this scheme and certainly not the last. As early as 1586 William Camden had actually published, in a single volume, a description of every county in Britain. His *Britannia*, first published in Latin, was enlarged and ultimately translated several times before his death in 1623, and then reappeared, yet further enlarged, on the crest of each wave of later antiquarian enthusiasm. Thus it was edited by Edmund Gibson, future Bishop of London, and a team of local correspondents in 1695; a century later the dilettante collector Richard Gough (1735–1809) produced a new edition in 1789, superseded by a three volume folio recension, also edited by Gough, in 1806. Each edition contained more on the history of individual manors and families, but even the last could not match the Lysons' ambitions to write a standard, if fairly brief, county history for everywhere from Bedfordshire to Yorkshire. Their books conform to the established pattern, with 'general' introductions followed by parochial histories. The series, which never came near completion, is probably most useful for counties such as Derbyshire which contrived never to have a 'classic' history produced by a local author.

After the efflorescence of antiquarianism in the period 1780–1830, which produced a vast and by no means wholly original literature, the next turning-point came in the middle decades of the nineteenth century with the building of the railways, the emergence of an educated middle class, the mechanisation of printing, and another intellectual revolution comparable to that of the sixteenth century.

All these developments profoundly changed the way in which local history (including field archaeology) was pursued. As well as destroying a great deal, the railways led, directly or indirectly, to the discovery of much archaeology. Cuttings sliced through prehistoric ditches and banks and exposed accumulations of worked flint; the lines that followed carried people in greater numbers than before and at less expense, on excursions to visit those monuments which were not obliterated. The people who went on these excursions were not so much the gentry who had hitherto written most local history, or the individual travellers who described their journeys in the earlier diaries. They were the clergy and the new professional classes created by the Industrial Revolution, especially architects, who contributed much to the careful recording of medieval buildings, as well as over-restoring village churches. These people were far more numerous than the eighteenth-century antiquaries and more gregarious. Above all, they joined societies: the second half of the nineteenth century saw the creation of most of the English county antiquarian societies which have since bulked so large in the promotion of local history, archaeology and, at least in the past, natural history. The Welsh county societies, it may be added, are mostly twentieth-century foundations, although the Cambrian Archaeological Association, covering the whole of Wales, is much older.

The archetypal county society of the later nineteenth century had its headquarters in the county town, where it would either rent rooms or, if it was lucky, acquire a convenient castle, as at Lewes or Taunton. The lord lieutenant would almost always be its president, and the diocesan bishop and other resident peers formed a bench of vice-presidents. The membership at large would be a combination of gentry, professional people and clergy. The society's aims would generally embrace natural history as well as archaeology and local history; its activities would include lectures and excursions, the publication of an annual report and transactions, the formation of a library and museum, and possibly also the appointment of a 'vigilance committee' to warn clergy against excessive church restoration. The growth of a new middle class created the clientèle of such societies; a long era of cheap printing that was to last up to 1914 enabled them to publish on a scale that few have been able to since.

The most enduring monuments to the county societies are their journals, which in most counties constitute, from around the 1860s or 1880s, a vast store of articles, long and short, good and bad, which are always worth searching for any large-scale community history today. Amid the derivative descriptions of churches and manor houses visited by the society the previous summer, and the lepidoptera report for 1891, will be found otherwise unpublished archaeological discoveries, transcripts of medieval charters now lost, and pedigrees of families on which no modern work has been done. As with the county history, the traditional county journal has little to say in its earlier numbers about, say, Victorian brickmaking, but for the village historian it remains a major source.

The period which saw the birth of most of the county societies was not such a productive age for the county history. A few societies made early attempts to produce collaborative volumes, but in general there was a realisation that the explosion of historical knowledge in the nineteenth century had at once rendered most county histories out of date and made their effective revision by one author impossible. This revolution in historical research stemmed partly from an early nineteenth-century concern for the preservation of Britain's immensely rich heritage of public records, evinced by the appointment of a succession of royal commissions from about 1800, and the establishment in 1838 of the Public Record Office as a home for millions of documents scattered between a variety of unsuitable repositories in different parts of London. Although little was done in this period for local records (except enquiries by the Record Commission about borough and quarter sessions records and John Rickman's attempts to abstract population data from parish registers), the creation of the PRO was a great stimulus to historical research and to the publication of transcripts or catalogues of the main classes of medieval administrative records. Ultimately, this led to a revolution in the way in which English history was written; at local level antiquaries could now re-examine many of the documents used by their seventeenth-century predecessors. As more material was published, first by the Record Commission, then by the Master of the Rolls (the titular head of the PRO), then by a growing number of national and local societies, so the printed sources for local history, even the narrowly conceived history of manorial descents, multiplied. As the nineteenth century wore on, a similar process led to the opening up of ecclesiastical archives for the first time and the publication of collections of medieval deeds (especially the cartularies of religious houses), all of which swelled the available material for a county history.

As local antiquaries abandoned ambitions to write county histories, so they became more concerned with individual parishes. In a sense, this reflected the changed social circumstances of the authors. Whereas a seventeenth-century gentleman saw the county as his natural frame of reference, a late nineteenth-century parson naturally settled for an account of the parish in which he had the cure of souls. Between about 1870 and 1914 dozens of parish histories were published, some as large as an early county history, others no more than enlarged church guides. Hundreds of smaller scale endeavours ended up in local journals. To help these new authors one of the most active, if not always most careful, of clerical antiquaries, John Charles Cox (1843–1919), produced a modest manual entitled *How to Write the History of a Parish* (1879), the first modern local history textbook; its scope amply demonstrates what was expected of the thorough parish historian of the day.

The climax of this Victorian heyday of antiquarianism, marked by so much new publication and by a much wider interest in the subject, came in 1899 with the launching of a project to equip every county in England (but not Wales) with a new history, still conceived on traditional lines but executed with a uniformity and thoroughness that even the Lysons never dreamt of. Instead of two men covering the whole of the country there was to be a team in every county producing uniform chapters, first for a series of 'general' volumes, and then for another series of parochial histories. When it was completed, the scheme would enable one to turn up an authoritative history of any parish in England, or a definitive account of the Roman remains, schools, religious houses or whatever (including natural history) of every county. The project was also designed to yield a substantial profit to its promoters, who secured royal approval to call it the 'Victoria History of the Counties of England'. Her majesty lived to see only one volume of VCH published, but the following hundred and more have all been dedicated to her memory.

Like the county journal, VCH is often among the first sources which the beginner comes across in his local library. For most counties, at least two volumes were published before the first war, usually completing the 'general' articles envisaged in the original plan; only for a few counties were the parish histories all published, usually by the 1920s. The early volumes usually provide the best available text of Domesday Book for the county (with introduction and translation), and useful if brief accounts of religious houses and the older schools. The archaeological articles are obviously out of date, but may still represent the most recent synthesis of knowledge. The chapters on political and economic history are very general, but the sections on individual industries can still be useful as a starting point. Like the county journals, VCH may seem old-fashioned but is still worth consulting.

The story of the Victoria County History project is very much a microcosm of how English local history has developed since 1900, even though since 1945 VCH and mainstream local history writing —academic and amateur—have moved progressively further apart. Before 1914 rapid progress was made with the new series, progress that came to an almost immediate halt with the outbreak of war. After 1918 the society which had supported so much antiquarian endeavour was greatly reduced in numbers and wealth; subscribers for schemes of all kind, VCH included, were much harder to find. The number of counties for which the History continued to be published fell; other publishing ventures ceased altogether. The county journals generally survived, although annual issues grew thinner. There was also an intellectual stagnation. Little was written that was new in approach: in most counties books and articles remained cast in a traditional mould and tackled traditional topics. There were no new projects for county histories outside the VCH scheme, except in some Welsh counties where substantial public subsidies were secured.

As in so many fields, it was only at the end of the second world war that a real revival in local history began. It took many forms, one of which, the work of W. G. Hoskins and his supporters at University College, Leicester, where a Department of English Local History was established in 1948, has already been mentioned. His *Local History in England* (1959) was highly influential in deciding how the subject was studied at all levels. Parallel with this new academic impetus, of which the revival of VCH in several counties was another aspect, came the establishment of a Standing Conference for Local History under the aegis of the National Council of Social Service. This was a federation of county committees, themselves made up of the new local history groups then springing up in towns and villages all over the country. Whereas the county societies, at least in England, are now mostly about a century old, the smaller groups which most local historians join first are rarely more than 30 years old and in many cases much less. Lacking the conservatism and what some would see as the pretensions of the county societies, these new groups were the spearhead of post-war amateur enthusiasm for local history. As they became established, their newsletters evolved into magazines, lecture meetings developed into group research projects, and many societies worked towards the publication of a collaborative town or village history.

A further important post-war stimulus to local research by amateurs was a great expansion of teaching by university extramural departments and other providers of adult education. Much of this remained traditional in that the audience simply listened to lectures, but some tutors led research groups which studied communities in depth, taking advantage of the capacity for a coordinated group of students to digest voluminous and possibly repetitive records much more quickly than could an individual on his own. V. H. T. Skipp has described work of this kind which he was pioneering in the West Midlands in the early 1950s; by the 1970s it had become a standard and very popular feature of most extramural programmes.

Research projects of this kind, whether by individuals or groups, led by societies or classes, would have been impossible had it not been for the establishment of a record office in virtually every county, many boroughs and some universities in the decade after 1945. Those offices which had been set up in the 1920s and 1930s enlarged their holdings both of administrative records and private deposits, especially estate papers, as there was a further round of country house sales after the war. The increased resources of record offices, coupled with the coming of cheap photocopying, greatly widened the scope for local history research from original documents housed other than in distant and inaccessible London repositories.

Under the influence of scholars such as Hoskins, and his successor at Leicester, H. P. R. Finberg, local historians since 1945 have studied a subject transformed out of all recognition since its last period of popularity at the end of the nineteenth century. The emphasis is now on the community as a whole: the landless as well as the landed; the poor as well as the rich; the nonconformist chapel as well as the parish church; trade and industry as well as farming; working-class suburbs as well as pleasant countryside. At the same time, the chronological scope has widened: local historians now pursue the early history of motor-car ownership as well as the history of coaching inns; the impact of the slump of the 1930s as well as the plague of the sixteenth century. Topography itself has enjoyed a new vogue as 'landscape history'. The study of past industry, using field evidence as well as documents, became intensely popular in the 1960s as 'industrial archaeology' but now seems to have lost some momentum. The memories of elderly residents are sought not, as used to be the case, for recollections of local customs or folk songs, but to capture on tape some idea of what domestic service was like before the Great War. All this is local history of one kind or another, and much of it, especially where the integration of visual and written evidence is concerned, has a longer history than some of its present practitioners realise.

One other renaissance should also be mentioned, although it does not really belong to the Leicester School. This is the quite extraordinary popularity currently enjoyed by genealogy, which has a long tradition but which in its new guise of 'family history' has attracted thousands of new enthusiasts, led to the establishment of dozens of new societies, and placed such pressure on certain classes of record office holdings that the staff have difficulty coping with it, and the very survival of the documents themselves is threatened. It remains to be seen whether this fashion passes, rather as that for industrial archaeology did, and what if anything it contributes to mainstream local history.

The explosion of interest in local history and its pursuit by amateur researchers, either alone or in groups, has created a correspondingly vast literature of newsletters, magazines, booklets and journal articles. In most counties, there are now several more popular magazines alongside the traditional county journal, offering an outlet for more modest pieces of research. Groups, individuals, record offices, extramural departments and others publish booklets embodying the results of research, or describing particular sources. The only overall guide to the progress of the subject remains a quarterly magazine, *The Local Historian*, founded privately in the early fifties but for most of its life published by the Standing Conference for Local History. The latter was remodelled in 1982 as the British Association for Local History, which remains the only national body for local historians generally and is now the publisher of *The Local Historian*. There are also numerous more specialised groups, such as the Society for Landscape Studies or the Association for Industrial Archaeology, as well as the much older Historical Association. The gregarious local historian has the choice in most counties of joining a traditional county society, which may on closer inspection prove less stuffy and pretentious than at first sight, or a smaller group in his own town or village. The latter also may be stuffy and pretentious, or it may do no more than hold lectures and excursions; more likely, however, is that it will contain a nucleus of keen members engaged in their own research or combining in a group project. The local group will probably publish a newsletter and possibly research papers; the county society will have a journal and probably some other publication. If neither seems likely to help, the would-be amateur researcher can join an evening class, preferably one where there will be opportunity to look at, if not actually work on, photocopies of documents. Few classes in fact now lack some element of practical work by students, and some are explicitly research based. If he lives near a suitable centre, the reasonably experienced amateur may be interested in working for a diploma or certificate in local history, such as several extramural departments offer; either will almost certainly require the preparation of a short dissertation based on original research.

If none of these opportunities for self-education appeals or is available in a particular place at the right time, the prospective local historian might do worse than read the rest of this book.

Chapter Two
AT THE LIBRARY

Making a start

People become interested in local history for many different reasons and their approach to the subject will vary accordingly. Someone investigating the comparatively recent past may well start by talking to older residents and not look at documents, maps or books at all. Others, especially those interested in genealogy or the history of their house, may have some of the source material—birth certificates or deeds—in their own possession. In general, however, most local historians, sooner rather than later, realise that their local library or record office is likely to have most of what they want and will accordingly present themselves at one or the other. Some researchers, with some idea of what they are doing and possibly in search of a specific type of record, will go at once to the county record office. The absolute beginner, or anyone with an interest in his community as a whole, will do much better to start with the resources of the local library and then investigate the record office. In principle, local studies libraries collect books, periodicals, pamphlets, maps, illustrations and printed ephemera relating to their area, while record offices are concerned with the archives of the authority which provides the service and with documents entrusted to their care by others. The divisions between libraries having printed secondary sources and record offices having primary manuscript material is not absolute—some libraries have large manuscript collections and all record offices have some printed books—but this is roughly how the material is divided.

Free public libraries are more than a century old in England and Wales and today provide a great variety of services to their ratepayers. The collection of local material is one of their older functions. It was the municipal authorities who first established libraries, the county councils following only after the first world war, and it was the boroughs and county boroughs that built up the largest local collections. Sometimes these were very comprehensive: the magnificent city libraries of Sheffield and Birmingham, for instance, have traditionally collected material relating to north

Derbyshire and south Staffordshire respectively, not merely their own authority's area. This sort of coverage is a legacy of the days when there was no public library service outside towns and cities and it was natural for a library in a county town to take in books and other material for the whole of the shire. After 1945 the county library services built up local collections, but, given the scarcity and value even then of most eighteenth- and nineteenth-century topography, they were unable to collect retrospectively to rival the holdings of the older collections. In many counties, the county library's local collection did not grow far beyond a limited range of modern material at headquarters.

This historical background is useful in understanding how local studies collections are arranged, because the distinction between borough and county holdings was blurred in 1974, outside the metropolitan counties, by the reorganisation of local government. District councils, except for four special cases in South Wales, do not provide library services, and so throughout the shire counties the older borough libraries became part of an enlarged county service. This transformed county libraries' holdings of local material and allowed many to think for the first time in terms of a coordinated service throughout their area. On the other hand, although all the local studies libraries of a county are now under a single authority, it is important to appreciate that each former borough library is likely to have some unique material for its immediate locality; that the main collection in the county will almost certainly have material for the whole of the area and not merely the county town; and that at least the largest of the old borough collections will be richer than a collection at county library headquarters, even if the latter is closest to the record office and thus seems the most convenient place to work. In some fortunate counties—for example Norfolk or Devon —the record office and library share premises, but more often, for historical reasons, they are widely separated.

General comments such as these cannot fully explain the various ways in which local studies collections are organised, but the local historian will soon work out how the system works in his own area. In a metropolitan county the main public library will usually have an old-established collection forming its own department with a number of professional staff, while the smaller district libraries may house theirs in the reference library with only one qualified (or even interested) librarian in charge of local material. In rural counties there may simply be the collection in the county town; in other non-metropolitan counties there will probably be a network of small and medium-sized collections in the former municipal boroughs.

Because of the wide variety of local studies libraries—large and small, well housed and cramped, well catalogued and neglected, regional and local—it is difficult to explain in detail what the local historian will find in his own area. Unless he has some experience of using specialised libraries already, he will probably feel over-whelmed on his first visit to a large city library and for this reason it is probably best to start with a local borough library. All such libraries should have many of the printed sources outlined in the preceding chapter: the classic county histories, whatever has been published of the Victoria County History, a complete run of the county journal, and much of the monograph and pamphlet literature published on the county. This is basic stuff and the local historian interested in his area as a whole, rather than a specific aspect of its history, should find plenty to be going on with in this material alone. VCH may, as explained in Chapter 1 (p. 20), be a disappointment except for supplying a reliable text of Domesday Book and perhaps a short history of the local grammar school, but if there is an older county history that should at least provide an outline history of the manor and a description of the church. The extent of finding-aids in the library will depend on how long the collection has been established and what resources have been available for its development, but most local collections have an index arranged by place, which should locate any published parish histories. It may also index articles, or there may be a separately published index in the county journal. In some counties, the library will have a series of local record society volumes, or a series published by the society that produces the main journal. These will be volumes of edited documents relating to the county, either transcribed at length or summarised ('calendared'). Again the volumes should be indexed: if you are interested in a particular parish try searching each index under that name. The older volumes will be concerned mainly with medieval documents and may contain lengthy stretches of untranslated Latin, but it is worth making a note of any reference to your parish for future use, even if you do not at first grasp exactly what the reference means.

The phrase 'making a note' raises the whole question of organising your material. Many visitors to a local studies library, or indeed a record office, have a very casual interest in what they are looking for and never pursue their enquiries after a first visit. Others do, and find that the notes they took early on in their work are so badly organised that they have to do much of it again. If you are interested in exploring the history of your parish, or some other topic, in any depth, possibly with an eye to eventual publication, it is worth taking from the start some very simple steps towards organising what you do properly.

The best way to start any local history research project is to buy a large pad of lined, margined A4 file paper and a file to keep it in. This may sound banal, but it is surprising how many people still start on the back of an envelope and then cannot make sense of what they wrote a month later. If the notes were made at a library some distance from home this is money as well as time wasted. A4 file paper is greatly superior to a spiral-bound 'reporters' pad or anything smaller, because the sheets can be filed. At first they will all go in one file, preferably with card-dividers to separate different subjects; later you will need several. A4 paper can be moved about between files; sheets stapled together in an exercise book cannot. Secondly, avoid the lure of the card-index. If you are starting work on a Ph.D. a packet of record cards and a box looks impressive but indexes soon become expensive and impossible to cart round to libraries and record offices. Cards also have a propensity to fall out all over the floor which is not shared by paper in a ring-file. Card-indexes have their uses in more advanced projects but are a luxury best avoided by the beginner.

What do you write on the paper, especially on your first visit to a library? A good plan is to start by searching whatever finding-aids are available and making a note of useful references, then to follow up the more obvious of these, such as articles in the county journal or a parish history. Keep a separate list of references and tick them off as you look at them. Some may be so specialised that you will not feel they are relevant, but it is worth keeping them for the future. The books and articles you trace are best listed in the same way as they appear on library catalogue cards or a computer-printed catalogue. There is no great mystery about the accurate presentation of bibliographical references and it does make it much easier to find things later. For a book you need the name of the author, the title and the date of publication, in that order. If you are requistioning material from a closed-access stack you will also need the class-mark, which in most public libraries will be a locally adapted version of the Dewey decimal system. For a journal, note the author and title of the article, the name of the journal and the year and date of publication. Some journals delight in making their citation as complicated as possible ('3rd series, XIII, Part 3, 1956 for 1949–50, Vol. 71 of the cumulative series' would be an extreme case) but it is important to know where a particular article can be found. Avoid the temptation just to note the title of the journal and the year: you will not remember a month later whether this was a passing reference or a substantial article.

Having got some references to look at, it is equally important to make notes from each book or article in an organised way. As far as possible, make notes from different sources, especially if they are on different subjects, on separate sheets. This will make more elaborate subdivision of your filing system easier later. What is vital is to repeat the bibliographical references at the head of the sheet, unless it is a very basic source, in which case the author's name will probably do. A local historian working in Nottinghamshire should find 'Thoroton' a sufficient reference to the main county history, and in any county notes from VCH can simply be so headed, rather than treating each chapter as an article. For articles proper, however, it is important to note author and title as well as the year and page of the journal. A second basic point is to note the *page* from which your notes are taken. This is essential if you wish ever to publish a properly annotated article and desirable if you wish to retrace your steps in the future. The margin of A4 file paper is well adapted to accommodate page numbers.

Once into this simple discipline, you should be able to work steadily through printed material relevant to your chosen topic, making notes whose source can be identified and noting references which a librarian can find for you. A few other points should perhaps be made at this stage. One is to beware of the temptations of the coin-operated photocopier which now stands in the corner of most local studies libraries. Certainly, cheap copying has revolutionised almost all kinds of historical research; in particular one no longer has to trace maps and drawings laboriously. In record offices it is a useful short-cut if you want one document from an office a hundred miles away or if it is going to take you an hour to struggle through a medieval deed. But in a library it is worth remembering that photocopiers do not actually read the books for you, and they certainly do not make intelligent notes on the bits that are relevant to your work. Simply to identify a dozen articles and get them all copied is not historical research, it is welcome income for the library and provides the researcher with a pile of copying which still has to be digested. Unless your opportunities to visit libraries are very restricted, try to sit there and read the stuff rather than rely too heavily on a copier. If you do make copies of particular pages—say of maps and illustrations—it is best to copy them on to the same A4 size paper as your notes, so that they can be filed together. Another rather obvious point is that very few if any public libraries lend material from the local collection because of its age and scarcity. Here it is worth investigating the book collection of the county society. Their 'library' may be just a cupboard somewhere in the public library (some are much larger) but for most counties you can still fit the basic printed sources into a cupboard and most societies allow members generous borrowing privileges. A £10 subscription may seem more reasonable if you establish what else you get for it besides a rather stodgy journal and six lectures a year at the other end of the county.

The library catalogue should give you a good start in any local history project, especially when coupled with advice from the staff, who in a local studies library have often been there a long time and know their collections well. Undoubtedly the simplest kind of enquiry to answer is one about a place, particularly a parish. The fundamental importance of the parish in local history will become more apparent when we look at archival sources (p. 47) but even for printed material it is still the unit under which information is most commonly organised in library catalogues. Searchers after specific subjects may have to think more carefully about how best to quarry out material in a library. For some topics, for example transport history, the catalogue should lead straight to a large local literature. For well known personalities, there should be an obituary notice if nothing else. The sort of enquiry that is much harder to answer is one about an obscure subject or a minor person or building. The genealogist or historian of his own house will rarely find ready-made references to either his grandfather or his home in a local collection catalogue: here the best advice is probably to 'think in parishes'. There may be nothing, according to the catalogue, on the history of your mid-nineteenth-century converted farmhouse, but the farm will certainly be mentioned in a directory and possibly in a descriptive article on the parish in which it lies. If it is of any architectural interest it will appear in the statutory list of buildings so designated, which is also arranged by parish. Likewise some Victorian worthy whose obituary fails to appear in a well indexed cuttings file may well be mentioned in a completely unindexed 300 page history of his home town published in 1901 and catalogued under the name of the place. Similar advice applies to local historians interested in minor industries. Nothing may have been written about basket-weaving in the county as a whole, but histories of particular parishes in which it once flourished may have snippets of information.

It will soon become clear to the local historian working in the library that, as was shown in Chapter 1, the literature of local history has been accumulating for a long time and that one writer has borrowed from another, with or without acknowledgement. Most modern work on local history, and most of the basic sources such as VCH and the county journal articles, contain bibliographical references and it is from these that the beginner, having exhausted the immediate scope of the library catalogue, will move on to more obscure material. Here some simple advice on technical problems may be helpful. Modern historical scholarship has erected over the last century a mighty apparatus for identifying sources in footnotes to scholarly works. Much of this jargon can be offputting to the beginner, especially the parts in Latin. For unscholarly references there is the added challenge of guessing what the author actually meant. Leaving on one side the citation of documents in record offices (p. 152), references to printed works should be given in the form explained above, either within the text itself or in a footnote. Problems stem from repetitive references where the writer has used the old fashioned formula 'Smith, *op. cit.*, p. 91' rather than what is now regarded as better modern practice, 'Smith, *Barsetshire*, p. 91'. Both refer back to a full reference to the standard history of Barsetshire, but whereas there will only be one Smith's *History and Antiquities of Barsetshire* there may be numerous works by people called Smith cited earlier in the book. '*Op. cit.*' merely means the work previously cited; its cousin '*art. cit.*' means a previously cited journal reference. The use of neither is to be encouraged: it is far better to use a short title for second and subsequent references. Likewise, it is a sign of pretentiousness for modern local historians to write '*V. supra* p. 1' when they want the reader to look back to the first page; in journals the phrase '*Ante*, XXV.16', referring to an article published in an earlier number, is also obsolete and a full author–title–year reference should be used instead. In the older county histories another Latin term likely to perplex the beginner is *penes*, as in 'Deed *penes* H. Smith gen.', which simply refers to a deed then in the possession of Mr Smith. What has happened to his deeds since 1750 is another problem.

Incomplete or obviously inaccurate references can often be identified by an experienced librarian, since the chances are they will be from one of the standard local histories; what may cause more difficulty are heavily abbreviated references to general published works. In VCH or a modern monograph such abbreviations will be explained, but the author of a parish history published in 1900 would have considered it an insult to his readers' intelligence actually to have explained what '*Val.Eccl.*V.504' meant. Most commonly, these will refer to published editions of medieval material in the Public Record Office, which tend to be available only in the larger public or university libraries (p. 130). The older county histories may contain even more obscure references to earlier editions of the same texts, or to manuscripts now in the PRO but accessible in published calendars. A brief guide to this is almost impossible and in practice most amateurs do not follow up references like 'Pat. 31 Ed. III° pars 1° rot.5d'. If necessary either a local librarian or the staff of the Public Record Office will translate this into modern usage and explain where to find it.

Gradually, the assiduous local historian will work backwards through a jungle of references and identify archive sources to be pursued in either local or national repositories. There is still, however, much to be gleaned from library material. Leaving aside maps, to which a separate chapter is devoted, and the manuscripts housed in some libraries (considered together with local record office collections), some of the most useful printed primary or semi-archival material in a library are those outlined in the next section.

Printed primary sources

One basic printed source which all beginners encounter is *trade directories*, classified lists of residents in each parish with a short descriptive introduction about the place. Directories first appeared in London at the end of the seventeenth century and spread to provincial towns and cities about a hundred years later. After various attempts, from the 1780s on, to publish a single national directory had proved largely unsuccessful a pattern emerged by the 1850s of county directories with a few national publishers, of which Kelly and White are the best known, and many local firms who issued a single town directory. The books are usually called *History, Directory and Gazetteer of Barsetshire* and follow a standard model. There is a short introduction on the county as a whole and then an entry for each place, usually by parish, sometimes with the parishes grouped by hundred, or (less conveniently) rural parishes clustered around market towns. For each there is an introductory 'history', the strictly historical parts of which, like the general introduction, usually come straight from the main county history and are wholly unoriginal. Lists of carrying and coach services (later railways and omnibuses), foundation dates of churches and chapels, an outline of local government (useful as this becomes more complicated after 1870), and details of acreage and population are much more valuable. Even if the information is to be checked later (e.g. the date of establishment of a gas-works from its authorising Act of Parliament) directories are a reasonably reliable short-cut to start with. The actual lists of residents are usually divided in nineteenth-century directories between the 'Nobility, Gentry and Clergy' and a classified list of tradesmen, from 'Academies and Schools' to 'Wine and Spirit Merchants', sometimes with the pubs and inns listed separately or with a final heading 'Miscellaneous', in which people like the gunsmith and artificial limb-maker of mid-nineteenth-century Brecon can be found.

Classified trade lists in directories are tremendously useful. They can be used to trace the career of one man or a family through several businesses, or (once houses in towns began to be numbered) the various occupiers of a single property. In the countryside they will usually supply a succession of tenants for a particular farm. So, of course, will census enumerators' books (p. 34), and more thoroughly, but directories are a quicker source of information. For the historian of a local industry, directories are much the best place to start, either for one business or for an industry over a wide area, rather than scanning maps, searching the census or (worst of all) expecting to find business records (see p. 67). For someone interested in a whole community, especially a rural parish or reasonably small town, a run of directories from about 1840 to the first world war provides a detailed introduction to nineteenth-century local history and an admirable springboard from which to move on to more specialised sources. After 1920 directories become less useful, as county volumes gave way to those covering several counties in which there was a single classified trade list for the whole region. Detailed local analysis is much harder, although one can still use the lists to trace individuals.

For a local historian or perhaps a group setting off on a fairly ambitious community study, a project worth considering is to take all the directories for a particular place, and to make a slip index of every entry in every edition. The resulting piles of slips can be sorted in at least three different ways. Arranged by trade they will provide a fairly complete census of local industry for much of the nineteenth century, from which one can trace the rise and fall of various types of employment. Arranged topographically in a town (in which houses are numbered) they will illustrate the changing character of each street (residential to professional; professional to commercial), as well as the history of each house. Arranged by name they will provide outline biographies of tradesmen and manufacturers' families over two or three generations. Even before this material is linked to maps or census records (pp. 72, 34), you have a good idea of what your community was like in Victorian times, down to the level of individual houses, businesses and families, which is satisfying in itself and should suggest further lines of enquiry.

Another basic source for nineteenth- and twentieth-century local history to be found in almost all local libraries is files of old *newspapers*. This is a much bulkier source than directories and its full exploitation is usually the work of years. The oldest provincial newspapers date from the eighteenth century, originating as a single folded sheet, with at least two of the four pages devoted to advertisements and much of the rest consisting of reprints from the London press. The earliest papers were regional rather than local and the amount of local news before about 1830 is limited. The advertisements can be useful in themselves but even a prolonged search of an eighteenth-century newspaper for references to a small village is unlikely to be very fruitful. For the history of the town in which the paper was published it will be more worthwhile, as will a search for a specific event which you know happened within say five years of a given date. Truly local newspapers, with a circulation covering only one town, sprang up mainly after stamp duty was repealed in 1860, and from then until the 1950s, when the local press went into a decline as costs rose faster than income, are a mine of information. Most towns could boast two or three rival papers up to the first world war; for local politics especially it is best to check all of them. During their late nineteenth-century heyday weekly papers were truly 'journals of record', with local authority meetings reported in great detail, speeches at official openings published verbatim, and court reports in full. For any aspect of a late Victorian town, especially crime and politics, newspapers are an inescapable source and far more informative than official records such as minute-books or court registers.

The disincentive to making extensive use of local newspapers is simply their bulk. If available in their original form they emerge from the stacks as large, often rather fragile bound volumes, pieces of which tend to come away in the hands of even the most careful reader. If produced on microfilm they are wearing to read for long periods, even on large-format viewers. It is notoriously easy to become side-tracked in making newspaper searches and almost as easy to miss relevant items. Victorian sub-editors did not favour eye-catching headlines or helpful cross-heads halfway down the column; the usual format was a solid block of very small type, often printed from a worn fount on poor paper. The best approach is probably to do a little at a time over a long period. Ask the library about indexes: some local studies departments, in the long-lost days of twenty years ago, had time to make subject indexes at least to their eighteenth-century holdings, which can save a great deal of time, as well as wear and tear on fragile volumes. Some evening classes have also tackled newspaper indexing projects and deposited the results in the library.

Another short-cut to exploiting local newspapers is to ask about cuttings files in the library. Compiling such files is another service for which there was more time in the past than today, and like indexing involves a fair amount of subjectivity as to what to cut out and which file to put it in, but even so such files can be extremely useful, especially if they are indexed. A file of obituaries, for instance, or one on local railway history, may well exist; other possibilities are cuttings of country house sale notices, or advertisements and news items concerning work on listed buildings.

Older local studies libraries may also have scrap-books of local *printed ephemera*, usually arranged by subject. As with most local studies librarianship, much depends on the vigilance, enthusiasm and workload of previous librarians, who had time to collect all the local theatre or football club programmes and put them into guard-books with production or team photographs alongside and possibly reviews and reports from local papers. A member of staff interested in railways may have gone out and taken large numbers of photographs in the early sixties as local branch lines were closed and stations demolished, putting them with press cuttings in a scrap-book of recent railway history. Someone may have given the library his comprehensive collection of local beermats, bottle labels and other ephemera of the licensed trade. This 'non-book' material, as librarians warily describe it, is not always fully catalogued but is worth asking about.

Two other categories of material in local libraries have already been touched on. One is the *photograph collection* which almost all old borough libraries have and which will have been exploited mercilessly over the last decade for *Grandfather's Barsetshire*, *Yesterday in Loamshire* and *Victorian and Edwardian Anywhere in Old Photographs*, apart from more specialised publications. Few local historians need to be told of the value of the old postcards, photographs, prints and engravings which make up the illustrations collections of local studies departments. They may be loose in folders or mounted in albums, they may be indexed or roughly sorted by place, they may form a full record to the present day or be strongest for the pre-1945 period. Some will include the results of systematic co-operation between the local camera club and the library to make sure that buildings are recorded before demolition; occasionally one finds (as in Cardiff) the very rich results of a similar project at the turn of the century. Whatever the scope of the collection it is almost always worth consulting, especially if it is indexed, and modern photocopiers can produce reasonably legible working copies of most material. For illustrations in publications a bromide copy will be needed, but few things liven up a history of Calvinistic Methodism in Blaencwm as much as a group portrait of the chapel deacons in 1932. It is worth remembering that most local museums also have photograph collections, and indeed collections of printed ephemera or other semi-archive material.

Most libraries (and museums) also have *manuscripts*. In some cases the material is similar to what would now normally be directed to county archive services, and it has ended up in libraries by historical accident (p. 42). One type of manuscript source, however, which when held locally tends to be found in a library rather than a record office, is the notes of earlier antiquaries. The collections of the major seventeenth- and eighteenth-century antiquaries are generally preserved nationally, especially in the British Library Department of Manuscripts (p. 141) or the Bodleian Library, Oxford (p. 144); county record offices may have acquired some material by purchase or in family deposits. But public libraries tend to be strongest in more recent collections, often very local in scope but sometimes extremely useful. Collections of this kind are an awful warning to present-day local historians of the danger of collecting notes unsystematically or never writing anything; some are a reminder of what large houses people used to live in, in which there were boxrooms that could literally be filled with boxes of grandfather's almost completed history of Barchester. For the local historian with fairly easy access to the library it is worth ploughing through dozens of school exercise books filled with neat longhand transcripts from the county history or scrap-books full of menus from pre-war Rotary dinners, because occasionally he will come across something original. It may be an obscure but accurate bibliographical reference, or a note that a local solicitor has all the papers of a particular family or business, or a record of what was on the site of Woolworths before 1950. Other antiquaries compiled card indexes of local biography or coats of arms or stained glass. There is always much dross in collections like this, but they are not usually very arduous to search and the results may be rewarding.

Census enumerators' books

Microfilm has already been mentioned as the means by which many libraries make old newspapers available to readers, while in some counties library catalogues are now printed on microfiche. The other major class of material which local historians use on microfilm are the enumerators' books of the nineteenth-century censuses, which are among the best known sources for genealogical research and a mine of information about any Victorian community. Strictly speaking, enumerators' books are part of the archives of central government and the originals are kept by the Public Record Office in London (p. 129). In practice, however, most local historians use microfilm copies of the books in their local library or record office (the whereabouts of the film varies between counties) and so it may most conveniently be described here. Because the material is relatively straightforward and yields large amounts of information without presenting many technical problems, it also fits into a chapter on 'how to get started' rather than one on more specialised sources at the PRO.

A census has been taken in Great Britain every tenth year since 1801, except in 1941. Until 1831 the enumeration consisted merely of a count by the overseers of the poor of the number of people (male and female), houses and families in each parish or township, with a simple attempt at occupational analysis. The establishment of the General Register Office in 1837 made it possible for the first time in 1841 to conduct a more sophisticated census, using the local officials of this department plus a large number of temporary employees, the enumerators. Since 1841 each householder has been required to complete a form given him by the enumerator a few days earlier on which he must list the name of everyone who spent 'census night' in his house, with certain information about each of them. In 1841 this merely included name, address, approximate age, occupation and whether or not the person was born in the same county as that in which he was then living. In 1851 the form was refined to include a column for marital status, the relationship of each person to the head of household, exact age, and parish and county of birth. The schedule of 1851 remained virtually unchanged down to 1881, the last year for which the books are open to inspection. (Since they contain personal detail, the books are closed for a hundred years from the date of the census, instead of the 30 years now normal for public records.)

In almost all counties it is possible to work on microfilm copies of the enumerators' books in a local repository and avoid a visit to London. The books are arranged according to the administrative geography of the Registrar General's department at the time of the census in question, in which the basic division of the country was into 'registration counties', which do not always correspond with geographical counties, and then superintendent registrars' districts, registrars' sub-districts and enumeration districts. In country areas the latter was usually a parish, or a parish might contain two districts; in towns a block of streets would be allocated to a single enumerator. In either case, the districts had to be small enough for one man to walk or ride round in a single evening, first distributing and then collecting the schedules completed by each householder. Having collected the forms and helped householders who were illiterate to fill them in, the enumerator copied each form into a book containing similarly ruled pages, drawing a line across the page after each household. At the front of the book were pages on which the boundaries of the enumeration district were described and the number of people enumerated on census night tabulated. The enumerator had also to explain any special surplus or deficiency of population in his district that night, such as the presence of railway navvies or the temporary removal of a platoon of soldiers. It has always been the Registrar General's policy to enumerate the *de facto* population of a district, rather than who 'should' have been there. Finally, the enumerator signed his book as being as correct as he could make it and sent it to the local registrar, who checked all the books for his district and sent them on to the superintendent. Eventually the books, now bearing three signatures as to accuracy, were forwarded to the Registrar General in London, where the numerical data (but not the nominal information) was analysed and the results published in a series of massive volumes presented to Parliament as sessional papers (p. 145). These reports, which are available in the larger public libraries, contain basic statistics for the population of every township and parish in the country, with more sophisticated figures on occupation and birthplace published for larger units, such as registration districts or counties. For the same information for smaller areas and for details of individuals one has to turn to the enumerators' books themselves.

The detail that can be extracted from the enumerators' books about a community of any size is almost endless, especially as five sets of books are now available, covering the period 1841–81. All the series are well preserved, although there are some gaps in the material for 1861 and occasional books missing for other years. For most purposes the 1841 census is less useful than the later ones because of the imprecise information collected about place of birth ('Were you born in this county, yes or no?', instead of 'Name the county and parish in which you were born') and imprecise age-reporting, where respondents had to give their age to the multiple of five next below their actual age (i.e. someone aged 69 would have reported his age as 65, as would someone aged 65, 66, 67 or 68). All the earlier books tend to give only approximate addresses for households, with no house-numbers in towns and no house-names in nucleated villages. Beginners should beware of mistaking the running household number in the left hand column of the page (i.e. the number that goes from 1 to n throughout the book) for a house-number, where the second column contains the name of a street.

Thus '60 Wellington Street' only means No 60, Wellington Street if all that information appears in the second column; if it is divided between the first two then 60 is the number of the household and the address is merely somewhere in Wellington Street. Apart from this trap, one of the attractions of the enumerators' books is the lack of technical problems. All the columns are clearly headed and the handwriting is usually fairly easy to read. Some occupations take a little effort to distinguish ('carrier' and 'currier', or 'chairwoman' and 'charwoman' for example) and phonetically spelt names of distant parishes in the birthplace column may require imagination as well as Bartholomew's *Gazetteer* to identify. The last column tends to be the least well completed, since many respondents believed that 'Ireland' was a county or that 'London' was a single parish. One also finds 'British Subject' in that column for people perhaps born to parents serving overseas during the Napoleonic Wars (1793–1815) who wished to make sure of their nationality. 'N.K.' for 'Not known' can occur for either the parish or county in the same column, and occasionally in other columns. Otherwise, abbreviations such as 'Ag.Lab.' for agricultural labourer or 'D.S.' for domestic servant soon become obvious, while professional qualifications (usually medical) reduced to abbreviations can be identified in a dictionary. Abbreviations for long disbanded service corps can be more of a problem. Sometimes, despite the care with which the census seems generally to have been taken, one finds obvious mistakes, such as the transposition of information between columns or a patently impossible combination of age, sex, marital status or occupation, which has escaped the notice of the Registrar General's checkers.

Some local historians use census records merely to locate their own or another family, since the returns contain such invaluable genealogical information as age and birthplace, as well as providing a cross-section picture of a complete household; or to discover who was living in their house on census-night in a particular year. Others may wish to use the books as part of a general study of a whole community, in which case they will probably do well to obtain a complete copy of the returns for their parish. Like the tithe map (p.77), the census enumerators' books are so useful that it is worth sinking some money into the acquisition of full copies. While for a small village one can transcribe the schedules of one census in perhaps an afternoon (preferably using a home-made form similar to the original), for a larger place photocopies are probably the answer. Many libraries and record offices now have microform readers which will also make 'hard copy', i.e. A4 or A3 photocopies from film or fiche. Prints of this kind from positive film (the only sort available from the PRO) are never as successful as those from negative stock, and some of the census film is now showing signs of age and over-use, but for most places it should be possible to produce legible working copies from locally held film. As always, avoid if possible ordering microprints from the PRO because of the extortionate cost. Local libraries sometimes need reassuring that the PRO is unconcerned about possible breach of crown copyright in the production of microprints from the census.

Having made a complete copy of one or more enumerators' books for your chosen area, whether it is a village, suburb or just a particularly interesting street, you can proceed in one of two directions. The statistically minded local historian may wish to produce figures for a small area comparable to those published for larger units in the census reports, such as the number of people born in different counties, a breakdown of the population by age and sex, or an occupational analysis of the community. This is a useful approach in identifying fairly precisely some of the leading features of a community (the importance of a particular trade in a one-industry town, or the number of Irish immigrants) but after a time diminishing returns set in. Average household size, for instance, while easy enough to calculate for anywhere from the enumerators' books, does not vary greatly between different parts of the country, nor did other aspects of family structure, for which results have been published for a number of large-scale studies and have been analysed through national samples. Your town or village is unlikely to differ very far from the norm, while for other variables (such as birthplace) your sample may be too small to be useful.

An alternative approach is to look at a community as individuals, rather than columns in a bar-chart or slices in a pie-chart. This one can do with a village or street, or, with group effort, a fair sized town. One can take all the members of a particular occupational group and see what common characteristics they had (were the farmers born locally? were railway navvies mostly Irish?); one can look at the social composition of particular streets (a high incidence of lodgers and an absence of servants indicating relatively low status, with these two indicators reversed suggesting high status); or one can look at migration patterns at individual level (e.g. a tenant farmer with several children all born in different parishes has obviously moved from farm to farm on annual tenancies and not been a long leaseholder at any). Almost all the information in an enumerator's book should suggest ideas to be explored in other ways (such as the prevailing type of farm tenancy in the last example), or to be examined over time by comparing one census with another. Another aspect of census analysis is to use the schedules in conjunction with a large-scale map of the district, most conveniently the tithe map for the 1841–51 period and the second edition of the Ordnance Survey for 1861 and later, making it possible to give a geographical dimension to each of the questions posed of the material. With a contemporary map one can also try to locate on the ground each household in the census, a task dignified in academic circles by the term 'house repopulation' but which in most amateur projects is simply an entertaining (and sometimes frustrating) exercise in seeing who one's neighbours were a century ago. Some of the practical difficulties of this work are outlined in the chapter on maps (pp. 85–6).

With this introduction to the incomparable wealth to be found in the census enumerators' books by the student of nineteenth-century local history we have now completed a brief tour of the material with which most local historians make a start. Some libraries will have more than what is described here, others will have less. In most parts of the country the resources of the nearest library can be supplemented by a major public library whose holdings are regional in scope. Occasionally a local university library may augment public library holdings, but in general the latter are the specialists in this field. Most local studies libraries have hand-outs on popular research topics, or simply on how to use the library; their neighbouring reference departments will have general books on subjects which you may wish to study locally; and the lending library should have the main local history, genealogical and archaeological textbooks. It is usually better to start research at the library rather than the record office: books are easier to read than most documents; library arrangement is more familiar to the beginner than the organisation of even a small record office; and you may as well see what other people have written about your parish before deciding what you are going to do yourself. On a more practical level, libraries tend to be open in the evening and for at least part of Saturday, which is when most amateur researchers can get into them; archive services generally work a five-day week. Finally, work on printed sources in a library, plus some of the semi-archival material described here, provides a good grounding in how to make notes, how to chase up references, and how to appreciate the way in which local historians draw on each other's work. Working in the opposite direction, one eventually gets back to a primary source reference to be followed up in a record office.

Chapter Three
AT THE RECORD OFFICE

Introduction

It is probably the current vigorous interest in genealogy which has done most to popularise the use of local record offices among local historians. Ten years ago many amateurs quietly pursuing the history of their village worked almost entirely in libraries and only visited the record office, with its awkward opening hours, to look at a few specific documents. Then came the deposit of parish registers, followed by large numbers of genealogical enquirers. Today almost all offices are under the sort of pressure which a few years ago afflicted only those which housed probate material and bishops' transcripts. It is unfortunate that this increase in demand coincided with the first period of real financial stress which most offices had known. Although archive services absorb only a tiny fraction of a county's budget they are seen by most authorities as fair-weather services, established when there was plenty of money and an easy target when economies are needed. As any county archivist will explain, it is much harder to cut five per cent off a small budget than a large one, since in his department that cut may be the salary of the only trained document repairer in the office, without whose services material in need of conservation cannot safely be produced to searchers. The first thing the local historian should appreciate about county record offices is that they are at the moment under unprecedented financial pressure, which is why some of them only open three days a week or try to charge you to look at the documents. In many offices the service to searchers is not what it was a few years ago.

Whereas most public libraries and their local collections are over a century old, the same is not true of county or city record offices. Concern about the preservation even of official local records followed well behind that for the archives of central government which prompted the establishment of the PRO in 1838. Only after 1918 did most county councils use powers they had possessed since 1889 to make provision for their own records and those of the general court of quarter sessions which preceded them. About a dozen counties set up record offices before the war, looking after the authority's own records, taking in material from defunct minor authorities, receiving some 'deposits' (i.e. long-term but revocable loans) of family and estate material or solicitors' papers, and possibly acting as the diocesan record office for the local bishop. After 1945 many more offices were established, until on the eve of local government reorganisation in 1974 the West Riding of Yorkshire had the unique distinction among English county councils (shared with some in Wales) of not providing an archive service. Since 1974 all the English counties except the West Midlands have maintained such a service and in Wales only Powys relies on an agency arrangement with the National Library.

The work of county record offices has grown enormously since pioneers such as F. G. Emmison were creating a new profession between the wars. It has not changed greatly in scope. A county record office exists partly to provide an efficient records management service for other departments of the county council, to select modern records of the authority for preservation and to make them available to searchers. In practice all county offices are also recognised by the Lord Chancellor as repositories for certain classes of what are legally 'public records' but are not kept centrally. The most important material of this kind is the records of *quarter sessions*, the partly administrative, partly judicial, body which until 1889 formed the top tier of local government in England and Wales and survived as a court until 1971. As well as looking after these, archive services have since 1974 taken into custody records of other local authorities in their area—mainly urban and rural district councils and county and municipal boroughs—whose successors, the district councils, do not normally provide record offices.

The second major category of local record office holdings is the records of the Church of England from *diocesan* (or in York provincial) level downwards. All bishops in England have now designated a local authority or university repository as their diocesan record office, to which have been transferred the administrative and judicial records of the bishop and of such bodies as the dean and chapter from the middle ages almost to the present. More recently, it has become the policy of the Church to encourage parishes to deposit their registers and other records in county offices, greatly accelerating a process that was already under way in many counties. In Wales the non-parochial records of the Church are deposited at the National Library at Aberystwyth, while parish registers may go either to the Library or, as is more commonly the case, to local offices. County record offices also have responsibility for inspecting and taking on deposit the records of 'civil parishes', the third-tier rural authorities set up in 1894, and the 'civil records of ecclesiastical parishes', which in many villages were not separated in 1894 from the church records as they were supposed to be.

Thirdly, local record offices receive on *deposit*, are given, or from time to time buy, a variety of other material. In particular they have received from the landowning families of the county collections of manorial records, estate papers, political and personal papers and much else. Such deposits often contain hundreds, if not thousands, of deeds, as do deposits from solicitors which form probably the second largest class of deposited documents in most offices. Record offices also take in material from nonconformist chapels, from trade unions and businesses, and from individuals. This material is so heterogeneous as to be impossible to describe briefly, but it would be true to say that the records of landownership bulk the largest among 'gifts, deposits and purchases'.

This outline of the collections of a typical county record office, like that of a local studies library, cannot explain in detail the considerable differences that exist between different counties. Some archive services run two or three branch offices, some do not have diocesan records, and all provide different levels of service to the public. In addition, some universities, and many local studies libraries and museums, especially in large cities, also have archive collections, mainly because these institutions were in existence long before county record offices and have collected manuscript material for many years. Thus in the West Riding, where there was no archive service, Sheffield City Library became the natural repository for several major estate and business collections, some of them of national importance, from the south of the county. In this case, the library established an archive department as well as a local history department; in smaller libraries the local studies section, or just an interested reference librarian, took in documents that would otherwise have been destroyed. An alternative course which was followed in some cities, for example Bristol, Southampton and Hull, was for the county borough to set up a record office within the clerk's department, initially to house its official records but also to take private material on deposit.

Local government reorganisation did not altogether accommodate the variations that had developed in archive services, and since 1974 the picture has become confused. In some counties which absorbed borough libraries with small archive collections these were quietly removed to county record offices. In the case of larger collections a record office may have sorted and listed archive material (possibly for the first time) without actually moving it. In metropolitan counties, city record offices and library archive departments have remained in existence alongside county council archive services. Because of these changes, documents said to be in libraries in pre-1974 references may now be in county record offices, and it would be true to say that in some borough libraries record office staff have made substantial new discoveries among un-catalogued documents. While there has been a slight tendency

among archivists to criticise the way in which librarians mana;
archive material before 1974 this should not obscure the fact that l...
the libraries not accepted the collections in the first place, perhaps
during a war-time salvage drive, or gone out to country houses after
the war and rescued tons of deeds and other papers, the documents
would not now be there to squabble over.

A first visit to a local record office is best prefaced not merely by
reading something about record offices in general and studying a
published guide or any leaflets the local office distributes through the
library service or otherwise, but also by making an appointment and
working out a fairly clear idea of what you want to see. It is
depressing for archivists to deal with searchers who have only come
to look at printed books on the search-room shelves which they
could see in their local library, or with people who haven't a clue
what they will find in a record office. No-one expects a beginner to
know exactly what he is looking for, or to have a thorough
knowledge of all the office's holdings; the trick is to ask intelligent
questions and to be able to ask for a couple of relevant things to start
with. For this, an initial exchange of letters or a telephone call is best;
in some offices it is virtually insisted on because of pressure on
seating or the need to bring documents to the office from some
distance. If you are interested in a rural parish, ask for brief details of
the main collections in the office which relate to the place. For larger
communities this approach can be unrealistic because the office will
have dozens of references and it is better to explain what aspect of the
town's history you are studying. For a particular industry, it is
reasonable to ask what there is in the office, although in some cases
this is either too general an enquiry (local offices in coalfields have
tons of ex-NCB records, mostly uncatalogued) or too specific (as in
the case of an enquiry about viticulture in Victorian Glamorgan,
which even the best arranged subject index would have had
difficulty answering). If you simply wish to confirm that a particular
set of parish registers is in the office, or a tithe map, a phone call is
enough to check that a seat will be available when you arrive, as well
as the document. It is unfair to ask archivists to answer detailed
enquiries over the phone, especially if they are on duty in the
search-room at the same time.

Most archive services work a standard office day and do not open
in the evenings or on Saturdays. For many local historians it is a
lengthy journey to the county town just to get to the office, so make
the most of your time. Arrive by appointment, preferably having
ordered a few documents to start with (most offices will only
produce a limited number at once). Do not come in even a small
group without prior authority. Do not bring sandwiches, typewriters or tape-recorders into the search-room, none of which will
be welcome. Bring one note-pad and several pencils, a rubber but
not your own pencil sharpener, because the droppings from it fall on

to documents and upset archivists. As soon as you arrive, have signed the visitors' book, found a seat and your documents, establish what local custom is for ordering more material. Some offices now only bring documents from the strongroom at set intervals; if this is the case in your office try to pace your work and have a supply of requisition slips ready to feed into the system, which will avoid the frustration of sitting there with nothing to look at while all around you are working away. All county record offices have certain common rules, with which the beginner should be familiar before his first visit. Apart from such obvious courtesies as not eating in the search-room or talking more than necessary (the reason for the rule in most offices that only one person may study a document at once), the most fundamental regulations concern the welfare of the documents. All material that is produced in the search-room must be handled with the greatest care. Bound volumes, especially parish registers because of the heavy demands made on them, should if possible be placed on stands rather than flat on a table; pages must be turned carefully. Under no circumstances should anything, especially sweaty hands but also notebooks, magnifying glasses or other impedimenta, be placed on the documents, which must not be piled on top of one another. If you are consulting a rolled map or any other document that will not lie flat of its own accord, the staff will supply paperweights. Boxes containing loose documents should be opened one at a time, to prevent mixing the contents. Above all, only pencil may be used to make notes and no mark of any kind may be made on a document under any circumstances. A few years ago, these rules were observed without comment in local record offices and search-room staff very rarely had to explain them to readers. Today, partly because of the influx of genealogical searchers with no previous experience of using record offices, staff frequently have to take positive action to prevent material in their care being abused.

Note-taking in record offices should be done in basically the same way as in libraries (p. 26), except that everything must be written in pencil. Head the page with the name of the office and then the reference number of the first document brought to you. The number will appear in a list or index and may be written on the document itself. Unless you are editing the document for publication there is usually no need to make a literal transcript of the text—merely note points of interest. If the document is a volume in which the leaves are paginated or foliated these numbers should be noted in the same way as the pages of the printed book, although for records arranged chronologically, e.g. parish registers, the date of an entry is probably a sufficient reference. As in a library, it is often a good idea to make a separate list of useful references from the finding aids and to tick them off as you look at them.

If you arrive at the office having written first to ask what is available for a particular topic you will already have some leads, or you may be following up footnotes in VCH or other printed sources. Once you have looked at any documents suggested by the archivist you will probably be shown the office's finding aids, from which already your initial enquiry will have been answered. The arrangement of documents in record offices does not vary fundamentally from county to county, but the extent to which holdings have been catalogued does, largely as a funciton of what staff are available and how long the office has been in existence.

The basic three-fold division of the holdings of most county record offices has already been described. This is normally reflected in the arrangement of the lists on the search-room shelves. The records of *quarter sessions* will most commonly be described first, then the *diocesan* records, then the *deposited* or transferred material. Some offices divide the last category by subject, so that there will be a series of lists of district council records, another of family and estate collections, one of business records and so on. Perhaps a more common system, although it may seem less helpful to the user, is for all the deposits to be numbered from 1 onwards (usually prefaced by D for Deposit), or to be given a mnemonic reference and the lists arranged alphabetically by this reference. Thus in Lincolnshire the muniments of Lord Ancaster have references beginning ANC, while in Nottinghamshire those of the Duke of Portland are DDP; by contrast Derbyshire and Staffordshire both use a running serial number system.

The official and diocesan records will be arranged according to 'administrative provenance'. Thus quarter sessions records are normally divided according to the particular task of the officer in charge (clerk of the peace, county treasurer, county surveyor and so on). The model arrangement of diocesan records followed by most offices is similar in character but disconcertingly complicated for the beginner. With the deposited records, gifts and purchases the fundamental principle is to keep each collection separate because of its separate provenance. Even if it consists of only one item it is not bulked together with other small accessions. Some collections of deposited material have a clear internal arrangement: this is normally true of local authority records or parish material. Alternatively, the material may have arrived not merely unsorted but disarranged, as in the case of a country house collection which spent the war in a leaking conservatory, or a solicitor's collection where different clients' papers have been mixed together on a strongroom floor. Here, apart from physically conserving the material, the archivist's task is to try to discern an order beneath the superficial chaos and catalogue the collection in that order. In an estate collection, deeds will be separated from rentals and surveys and usually arranged by place; official correspondence about the lord lieutenancy will be listed separately from private letters.

Once a collection has been sorted the next step is to list it, although some offices have a large backlog of unlisted collections. Completed lists are put on the search-room shelves (except in the case of modern or confidential records not immediately available to the public) and it is these the searcher consults. Search-room lists vary a great deal in the amount of detail they provide as to the contents of the collection, but as a minimum will give the searcher a reference number by which to order a particular item and probably some idea of its contents. A 'piece' thus ordered may be a volume, a sheet of paper or a parchment roll, a file or a photograph. On the other hand, a list is not the same thing as a 'calendar', a detailed summary of the contents of a document. In the case of most deposited material, a list should provide sufficient information for the searcher to establish whether it is likely to be useful. Thus a list of business records (say ledgers or letter-books) will give the covering dates of each volume. Rent rolls in an estate collection will be listed so that one can see which parishes or manors are covered.

In one particular case a search-room list may be sufficiently detailed to make it unnecessary to send for the original. This is where a collection of deeds has been listed so as to include everything useful in the original document. Most offices try to list medieval deeds in this way, because few searchers can read the originals (which are in Latin in a difficult hand). For later deeds, some collections may have been treated in the same detail, but few offices can go through large bundles of eighteenth- and nineteenth-century deeds in this way. They may merely note the parties to each deed and the places mentioned, or only prepare a list which identifies the contents of each box ('Bedfordshire, 1650–1900; Bucks, Medieval—c.1550', and so on). Here the searcher has no choice but to get the box out and go through it piece by piece.

Some local historians using county record offices are interested in particular subjects across all or part of the county; for them a folder of lists bringing together all the UDC records may be exactly what they want for their study of late nineteenth-century local government. If, however, they are working in an office which does not arrange its lists by subject, such searchers will have to rely on a subject index, usually on cards near the lists, to identify relevant collections. However the deposited records are arranged, the searcher interested in a particular parish or family will turn first not to the lists, unless he has been given some leads by the staff, but to the personal and place-name indexes. In an ideal office, all the names and places which appear in the lists will have been indexed, and all the collections will have been listed. In most offices, by no means all the collections have been listed, and by no means all the lists have been indexed. But as a start, look at the index under the place or person in which you are interested and follow the references there back to the relevant list. If the description in the list suggests the document will be useful send for it. (Archivists generally do not care for searchers who copy references from the index straight onto requisition slips; check the context first).

Much of this chapter has so far been devoted to how a record office organises its holdings, because this is precisely what a visitor to the search-room sometimes fails to understand. Record offices do not house a mass of undifferentiated documents out of which archivists somehow produce what you are looking for, or tell you they have nothing relevant; their holdings have come into the office from a variety of sources, some have been examined in more detail than others, and some parts of the county will be better documented than others. The lists and indexes are a partial but not complete guide. For example, just because a particular person does not appear in the name index this does not mean that there is nothing about him in the office. If he was a criminal he may feature in quarter sessions records, which are unlikely to be fully indexed by name; if he was a pauper, there may be an unindexed removal order in a parish collection; if he had business dealings with a firm whose records are in the office, he may appear in their ledgers. The same is true of any parish in the county. It is certainly the case that some parishes have better family and estate collections than others, and not all parish registers are equally well preserved. But all parishes feature in quarter sessions records and there will be something about most country parishes in the records of the relevant rural district council. To make full use of a county record office one must appreciate how its contents have come to be there, to what extent they have been catalogued, and above all the background history of the place, person or subject you are interested in, and the history of local administration which has created the records that are now in the office.

It would be impossible, even if the whole of this book were devoted to the holdings of the local record office, to go into great detail about the sources to be found there for every possible topic which a local historian might wish to pursue. What is perhaps best, in a book aimed at beginners, is to concentrate on a limited number of basic sources which present comparatively few technical problems and from which one can discover a good deal fairly quickly about almost anywhere, urban or rural. The focus in this section is mainly the parish, which remains the most meaningful unit in country areas to the present day for local administration and life generally. This is no longer the case in towns or in villages which have become suburbs, but until the nineteenth century the parish, despite its obvious inadequacy in many areas, was still the only unit of local government below the county and the one through which quarter sessions and central government exercised policy or collected information. At an early stage in any project, whether it is the general history of a community or something more specific, it is important to establish the parochial geography of the area you are interested in. Library and record office catalogues are usually arranged by parish, as are many general printed sources. An important qualification to this emphasis is necessary in the North of England and much of Wales, where the civil functions of ecclesiastical parishes (relief of the poor, maintenance of roads) were discharged by subdivisions of parishes called 'townships' in England and 'hamlets' in Wales. Often it was they, and not the vast sprawling parishes, which were the fundamental units of local organisation.

Another basic point is that it is unwise to think in terms, rather as J. C. Cox's manual did, of writing a continuous history of your parish from 1086 to the present. For most parishes there is very little material in local record offices before 1550; what there is is probably written in Latin and well beyond the expertise of most amateurs. Usually, what can be discovered of their medieval history derives from central government archives. For the 'early modern' period, say from 1550 to about 1750, there is a wealth of material in English local record offices, much less in Wales, but although most records were by then kept in English they are still written in a hand that needs some practice to master, especially before 1660. It may be fun to learn 'secretary hand' in an evening class from clear examples explained by a good tutor; it is rather dispiriting for a beginner to be given a document in a record office of which he is unable to read a single word, or to spend pounds on photocopies of sixteenth-century material which after hours of study still remains largely baffling. It is much better to start with straightforward post-1750 documents and to work backwards rather than forwards. Archive material from this period also ties in more readily with what the beginner is likely to have gleaned from printed sources.

Local administration

As good a starting point as any is probably local government records. Leaving aside for a moment the medieval chartered boroughs, some of which survived into modern times as local authorities and may offer rather richer source material for old towns, local government before the mid-nineteenth century was undertaken by two main agencies: the *county*, through quarter sessions, and the *parish* (or *township*). While it is worth checking any indexes to quarter sessions material that are available it is probably best to start with the parish and then look at the new statutory undertakings which replaced it during the nineteenth century.

Since early medieval times the whole of England has been divided into parishes, forming the lowest tier in a hierarchy of ecclesiastical administration that leads through the rural deanery to the arch-deaconry, the diocese and thence the provinces of Canterbury and York. Its best known records are the registers ordered to be kept in 1538 of all baptisms, burials and marriages in the parish, which have long formed the staple diet of genealogists and more recently have been extensively used for work on local population history. Only in a comparatively small number of parishes do registers survive from 1538, although for many English parishes they start before 1600. In Wales the starting date may be as late as 1750. Their use in genealogy or population history is well explained in more specialised books; their value for more general community studies is usually rather limited, unless the earlier volumes contain a good deal of annotation as well as simply recording vital events.

In the sixteenth century the parish (or township) was adopted by parliament as the unit within which two basic aspects of local administration were to be discharged: the relief of the poor and the upkeep of the highways. In each parish unpaid officials were appointed annually as overseers of the poor and surveyor of highways, in addition to the two churchwardens who were responsible, with the incumbent, for the maintenance of the church itself. A parish constable was also appointed with nominal responsibilities for law and order and a rather more real one for central government tax collection, in a hierarchy of civil officers which passed through the high constable of each hundred (or wapentake) and the sheriff of the county to the Exchequer in London, where the records of his work have ended up. Each of these four sets of officers had power to levy a rate to support their work, and all were supposed to keep accounts of its collection and disbursement. For the overseers this meant paying out dole to the poor, meeting the expense of removing as many paupers as possible to another parish, and perhaps in the eighteenth century contributing to the maintenance of a local workhouse. The surveyor's accounts either list payments to contractors for repair of roads, paid out of the rates, or record work done by ratepayers themselves to save the expense of paying outside labour. The churchwardens disbursed their rates not merely on routine items such as washing cassocks or paying for polecats to be removed from the steeple, but from time to time had to pay for major repairs to the church or even partial rebuilding, in which case the accounts may give the name of an architect. Constables' accounts usually record only the routine expenses of office.

Accounts such as these may survive from the sixteenth or seventeenth century in well documented parishes; even in less fortunate places there should be some material for the last few decades of the system. The poor law was reformed in 1834, highways administration a year later, while compulsory church rates, which the wardens collected and disbursed, ended in 1868. While the outgoings in any surviving account books illustrate how the parish was administered by its unpaid and often reluctant officials, the lists of ratepayers (by the nineteenth century kept in separate ratebooks) are sometimes useful in identifying who was living in specific, fairly substantial, houses which are named separately in the lists. Quite commonly, prior to about 1820, all the parish accounts were kept in a single book (the 'township book' in some northern parishes) and the same small group of men discharged all the offices year after year.

The various officials were responsible to a general meeting of parishioners, known from its nominal meeting place as 'the vestry', although meetings were often adjourned to a pub. Anyone, whether or not he was a churchgoer, could attend the vestry until its reorganisation in 1920, but usually only a handful of families were represented. In the early nineteenth century, especially in industrialising parishes, ratepayers realised that some sort of executive was needed to make parochial legislation work and a 'select vestry' evolved, acting as a *de facto* local council for what may by this date have been quite a large town. Such bodies, which varied from the highly efficient to the hopelessly corrupt, usually kept minutes, as did some ordinary vestries by the eighteenth century, and through these one can trace the efforts of the ratepayers to organise local administration. From the 1830s onwards, however, new bodies gradually removed all effective power from the parishes.

Before outlining the material likely to be available for later nineteenth-century local government it may be worth saying something about the most strictly ecclesiastical records of parishes besides registers. As they lost their general administrative functions to elected councils, Anglican parishes became far more energetic in their cure of souls, and this is often reflected in their archives. The middle decades of the century saw a great deal of church restoration, the building of mission churches, the division of over-large parishes into new districts, and the founding of church schools. This may have left a legacy of minute books (of building committees, restoration committees or school managers), accounts, or printed ephemera recording the laying of foundation stones or the opening of new buildings. It may be of interest to see, using directories in conjunction with parish records, what sort of people were supporting the church in this work; where nonconformist records also survive from the same community one can compare the progress of church and chapel and identify who supported which party.

The first major reform of local government concerned the *poor law*, which especially in southern England became the target of much well merited abuse in the early nineteenth century. In an effort to reduce rates and make the system more efficient, responsibility (except for actually collecting the rates) was removed from parishes to elected 'boards of guardians of the poor' serving a 'union' of parishes. This body was made responsible for building and running a 'union workhouse', usually in a local town, to which surrounding rural parishes were to send their poor. Outdoor relief was in fact never entirely ended and the system was greatly modified before its final abolition in 1930, when the guardians' powers (and thus their records) passed to county or county borough councils, while the workhouses typically became hospitals. County record offices will generally have, for most of the unions in their area, minutes and possibly other records from shortly after 1834 to 1930. From the minutes one can see the earliest of the new local government bodies working to enforce the Poor Law Amendment Act in their union, building a workhouse, appointing a master and matron, establishing policy and adapting to later legislative changes. For the workhouse itself there may be such human documents as diet sheets or admission and discharge books listing inmates who passed through the institution. While the interest of this material for the historian of a rural parish on the edge of the union may be limited, for anyone working on a town in which a workhouse was situated guardians' minutes are of value not merely for their administrative content but also because they recapture the political life of the time. Election contests can be followed in local newspapers as well as the minutes of the board.

The pattern set by the Poor Law Amendment Act, of a small central government department overseeing the work of elected local boards charged with a single task, was followed later in the nineteenth century by reforms in other areas of social policy. One such field, which again creates a large body of readily accessible material for the local historian, is *education*. Although the government, through a committee of the Privy Council, had been disbursing grants from the 1830s to voluntary bodies (Church and nonconformist) working to make elementary education more widely available, it was only in 1870 that an Act provided for the creation of elected school boards in places where voluntary provision was inadequate. Later in the nineteenth century elementary education was made first compulsory and then free, and it became clear that rate-supported schools would become the main providers of mass education, replacing voluntary bodies. It also became clear that the local school boards, whose view of their function often remained depressingly narrow, should be replaced by larger bodies. Thus in 1902 the education committees of county and county borough councils, and of the larger municipal boroughs and urban district councils, took the place of school boards. The minor authorities survived the reform of 1944 but in 1974 education was placed entirely in the hands of the county councils, except in the metropolitan counties, so that most surviving records should now have reached county record offices.

School board records, like most local government material, consist of minutes, sometimes interspersed with annual reports of the clerk to the board (the predecessor of the post-1902 education officer), from which one can study the struggle to provide a universal system of elementary education between the 1870s and the beginning of the present century. The proposed creation of a school board under the 1870 Act often triggered a great deal of local strife, as ratepayers fought to keep out yet another rate-supported body, Churchmen fought against 'secular' elementary education, and nonconformists wanted to establish schools run other than by Anglicans. As with guardians' elections, it is worth pursuing school board politics through the local press, especially at times when it is obvious from the minutes that there was bitter conflict on the board. Occasionally, where the records of a Church school have survived, it may be possible to look at both sides of a conflict, as the Church party fought first to prevent the creation of a school board, then to secure a majority on the board, and last of all to obstruct its attempts to take over Church schools.

Material may also have reached the county record office from the schools themselves, usually in the form of log-books kept by head teachers and returned to the authority when the school shut. Log-books provide a colourful picture of late nineteenth-century school life and have been the mainstay of many centenary histories, although in some counties they are closed for longer than the usual 30 years because of the personal nature of the contents. Schools that are still open sometimes retain their log-books, although increasingly these too are being transferred to record offices for safekeeping and ease of consultation.

Poor Law and education were two fields in which specially elected bodies were established by Parliament; while they were evolving there was a parallel process, concerned initially with *public health* reform, which gradually broaded into the kind of modern local government below county level that was swept away in 1974.

The first effective Public Health Act dates from 1848. It was adoptive, that is, ratepayers could choose whether or not to establish a local board of health. Most did not, except in the new industrial towns where the vestry was now ineffective as a local authority. Here, and in some older towns where a chartered borough became the local board, the Act was adopted and a board elected whose minutes may survive from soon after 1848. So also should a report on the health of the district prepared as part of the setting-up process, which often provides a comprehensive and lurid account of ill-health, poor housing, insanitary draining and administrative inaction. These reports were printed and may be found in local libraries as well as record offices; the Department of Health and Social Security (as the successor central government department) also has a set. Neither the initiative of 1848, nor a later Act of 1858, was universally adopted and it was only in 1875 that the first comprehensive Public Health Act established local sanitary authorities throughout the country. In rural areas the poor law guardians were at first responsible for public health under the Act, but in small towns, mining or industrial villages, or new suburbs where more action was needed, new 'local boards' were elected. Despite their title, they were at first concerned mainly with public health and only in 1894, when they were remodelled by the Local Government Act into *urban* and *rural district councils*, did they take on wider responsibilities. The largest became elementary education authorities in 1902; all acquired housing powers at the turn of the century.

UDC and RDC records were some of the bulkiest new accessions received by county record offices at reorganisation, even allowing for the amount that were destroyed either by retiring members and officers bitter at their councils' abolition or by archivists overwhelmed by furniture vans full of ratebooks. Since 1974 they have probably been among the least used modern records in local offices, and have been seen as distinctly unglamorous. The old district councils were not for the most part very exciting institutions; few of them spent ratepayers' money with the abandon of their successors and their records may seem of little interest. But it is worth checking from a directory when the local board in a small town or mining village was established and, especially if it goes back prior to 1894, trying to search out its minutes. Once again, one can identify the personalities behind early local government and retrace the struggle to clean up industrial communities in the late nineteenth century.

Two other new authorities may be mentioned here briefly: the *county councils* established by the Local Government Act of 1888 and the *civil parish councils* set up in 1894. County council minutes and reports (except early 'verbatim proceedings') are usually too general to be of interest to historians of particular communities; conversely the powers given to parish councils were so limited that their records, even though very local in character, rarely contain much of interest. The county councils celebrated their first half century in 1939 by producing a set of uniform handbooks, half of each book containing a standard account of county government since 1889 cast in the 'Fifty Glorious Years' mould, and the second half consisting of short accounts of each major committee of the authority whose name and arms were stamped on the front cover. They are interesting period pieces, still to be bought fairly cheaply, and a useful guide to the pre-war functions and outlook of the county councils.

Those towns which trace their administrative history from a medieval *borough* charter stand a little apart from the local authorities so far described, although their modern records are largely similar. Despite their mayor and aldermen, separate commission of the peace, ancient charters and coats of arms, all of which counted for naught in 1974, most trace their modern history from the adoption of the 1848 Public Health Act or one of the later reforms. The Municipal Corporations Act of 1835 merely provided for a proper system of election of members, appointment of officers and audit of accounts. Except for police powers, it did not lay new duties on the boroughs. Before 1835 surviving borough records may include minutes of some kind of 'town council', which may go under a variety of names; accounts; and deeds and other papers concerned with borough property. Few boroughs enjoyed much administrative vitality in the eighteenth century, even those that had their own court of quarter sessions, and their records tend to be correspondingly dull. For the larger towns of pre-industrial England, and a few of the smaller boroughs, there may be very rich early modern material in a city or county record office, as well as medieval charters establishing the burgesses' privileges in the first place. This has usually been well catalogued and is often partly accessible in print through local record publications.

The records of the statutory local authorities, especially for a small town or a suburb, provide a good picture of how nineteenth-century administration worked and amplify a picture of the community obtained from printed sources. Before going any further back, the local historian seeking material on an urban community, and to a lesser extent a rural parish, can check whether the county record office has received any deposits from other nineteenth-century institutions, such as nonconformist churches, trade union branches or friendly societies. This material, which is roughly similar in character to that created by local authorities but less bulky and less well preserved, will further enlarge the local historian's view of the last century of life in the community he is studying, without requiring any special expertise in reading the documents or understanding their contents.

Landownership and the history of houses

Having exhausted the scope of administrative records, the local historian may well turn next to the mass of material generated by landownership, whether of rural or urban property, which bulks very large in the holdings of all county record offices. Here the essential starting-point is to find out who owned the land in the parish in which you are interested. This can be done quickly from a directory or more thoroughly from the tithe map of the 1840s (p. 77) which will be available for most parishes. From here it may be possible to progress anywhere or nowhere. The pattern of landownership in the nineteenth century varied greatly between different parts of England and Wales, and within the same county. The most fortunate case is one where a single family enjoyed a long ownership, preferably including the lordship of the manor, of most or all of a parish, a family which has since disposed of its property and handed over estate papers to the record office. This is by no means a common state of affairs. Even if landownership was dominated by a single family, its records may have been largely or wholly destroyed. Even if it has well preserved muniments they may still be at the estate office, at which local historians may or may not be welcome. Alternatively, the parish may have been a peripheral part of an estate centred in another part of the country, with the muniments of the entire estate being deposited in a distant county record office. This problem especially afflicts parts of Wales dominated by English landlords: estate records for the town of Brecon have for this reason ended up in the Kent Archives Office at Maidstone, a strong deterrent to their use by local historians in Breconshire. Another possibility is that the crown, through the Duchy of Lancaster or Duchy of Cornwall for example, has been the major historic landowner. The muniments of both are kept in London (p. 136). The nineteenth-century owner may have been a recent purchaser of an estate and have inherited or kept nothing belonging to his predecessor. The parish may have been fairly evenly divided between several middling estates, none of which have much in the way of surviving muniments, or the parish may have lacked any dominant landowner but had numerous resident freeholders. These are all points worth bearing in mind before berating the staff of the record office for failing to have any family and estate material for your parish.

Personal enquiry and a search of the indexes should locate any estate material at the local record office; often the staff will know from previous enquiries whether there are any collections elsewhere or, if muniments are still in private hands, will advise on how, if at all, the owner should be approached for access. A more systematic way of obtaining the same two pieces of information is to write to the National Register of Archives (Quality Court, Chancery Lane, London WC2). This is a small official body which does not collect material itself but builds up lists of collections, either through the work of its staff or in collaboration with record repositories, and can help in tracking down fugitive archives. If you are specifically interested in locating manorial records (with which in practice are often to be found other records of landownership) ask for details (of particular parishes) from the NRA's Register of Manorial Documents. For anyone with the chance to visit London, all this can be done in person at Quality Court during office hours.

Assuming there is an estate collection in the local record office for your parish, what is it likely to contain? A good collection of this kind should include *deeds* recording the purchase or disposal of all or part of the estate; leases to tenants of land and farms within it; rentals listing tenants, their holdings, the terms on which the premises were held, and the rents paid; and, if you are lucky, estate maps. These will be mentioned more fully in the next chapter (p. 90) but are generally on a large scale marking individual fields, which are numbered and keyed to a written survey ('terrier') either alongside or separately bound. From this you can get an overall view of the estate at a particular date, and if you are very lucky there may be two or three such surveys a generation apart, enabling you to compare the growth or decline of the estate, or the appearance or disappearance of buildings, even of whole villages. If the map has been lost but the terriers remain, it should still be possible to look at change on the estate by comparing farm sizes and tenants' names. If one of the surveys dates from the 1840s or later it should be possible to compare it with both the tithe map and one of the sets of census enumerators' books (pp. 77, 34) to build up a very full picture of the estate in the mid-nineteenth century. To do this thoroughly really involves transcribing the entire survey and having any estate maps copied. The names of the tenants and their holdings can then be matched against other references, this being another instance, as with information from directories, where a slip index may be useful.

This sort of analysis should enable a whole parish, or a large part of it, to be studied in some detail, particularly for the eighteenth and nineteenth centuries. The same sources used in a more limited way can also help those interested in tracing the history of their own (or anyone else's) house.

Depending on the detail with which rentals and surveys have been compiled, it may be possible to link deeds from elsewhere in the collection with holdings listed in other records. The leases by which tenants held their property may survive (and can be linked to rentals by checking names of parties and farms); some surveys may identify from whom the estate acquired the property while the deed recording this conveyance may also be preserved.

All record offices have large quantities of deeds, mainly acquired from solicitors, which are not part of an estate collection but may include property in the parish in which you are interested. Make a note of the basic details of the deed and see if at some stage you can identify the property on a large-scale map or in a rental or survey. As suggested above (p. 46) it is often possible to rely merely on a record office list for the salient points of a deed, much of which is common form. There is a good published guide to title deeds (by A. A. Dibben) but three of the most common types of post-medieval conveyance should perhaps briefly be explained here. A freehold conveyance, that is, outright sale from A to B, was most often effected from the sixteenth to the nineteenth centuries by one of two procedures: bargain and sale or (in the second half of the period) lease and release. In both, the deed opens with the date and the names of the parties, in simple cases the name of the vendor followed by the name of the purchaser. Then comes the 'consideration', i.e. the price paid for the property, followed by the clause which defines the type of conveyance (bargain and sale or lease and release), followed by a description of the property, usually introduced by the phrase 'All that. . .'. When you come to the next standard formula, 'To have and to hold . . .' you can very often stop, since, mortgages and settlements apart, the rest is common form. The two types of freehold conveyance differed in phrase but not in intent. A bargain and sale was the more straightforward and was what its name implied; a lease and release was slightly more devious, consisting of a lease (i.e. the disposal of the property for a temporary period, in this case usually a year), followed a day later by a 'release' in which (in simple terms) the lessor of the previous day's deed gave up his right to recover the property from the lessee, making the conveyance equivalent to a bargain and sale. The two deeds were normally folded one inside the other; problems occasionally arise in spotting that a lease is in fact the preminary to a release when the latter has been lost.

The third type of document found very commonly in solicitors' or estate collections is a lease in the normal sense, in which a landowner let property either for a year or a term of years (commonly seven or a multiple thereof) or for a term of lives (usually three). Here the lease opens in the same way as a freehold conveyance with the date, names of the parties and description of the property, the latter preceded by the formula 'Hath sett to farm' or 'hath to farm let', which confirms that the document is a lease. Then will come the period for which the lease is to run and the annual rent, followed by 'reservations' to the landlord (most often of woods and minerals on or under the property) and then other special conditions ('covenants'). If the term of the lease is very long (999 years, or even 2,000, as occurs occasionally) the conveyance amounts to a sale of the freehold, even though the deed may be cast in the form of a lease.

There are numerous other types of title deed, and the documents tend progressively to become physically larger and more complex up to the end of the nineteenth century, and thus more offputting to the beginner. If they have not been listed in detail, either ignore them, or sit in front of them with Alan Dibben's booklet or an archivist with time to spare, until the important features begin to stand out from the common form. As already explained, medieval deeds written in Latin are usually calendared in full by record offices and may well have been published by record societies or munificent nineteenth-century owners.

Another class of material connected with landownership which people usually find hard going when first confronted with them are *manorial records*, especially the proceedings of manor courts. Again, medieval court rolls, if they survive, will either have been published or will, frankly, be beyond most amateurs; but it is not always appreciated that manorial land tenure ('copyhold' or 'customary-hold') survived until 1925 and in some parts of the country remained widely used. The tenure was called copyhold because the tenant's title to his holding was an extract from the manor court roll recording his admittance to the farm or other property, i.e. a copy of the roll. The alternative name arose because the property was held 'according to the custom of the manor'. Copyhold conveyances, i.e. brief extracts from court rolls recording the date of the conveyance and the names of the outgoing and incoming tenants turn up among the deeds to many properties; what is generally more valuable is the survival down to modern times of the complete rolls (usually in fact bound volumes by the nineteenth century) for a manor, in which all such conveyances are listed in chronological order. In parishes where most of the land remained copyhold or customaryhold until 1925 (instead of being converted to leasehold or tenancies at will) a long run of court books amounts to a miniature land registry for the parish. Here again, as with other bulky, repetitive sources, it may be necessary to note the details of each conveyance on slips or cards so that they can be sorted by party and by holding to follow either the history of a particular farm or the career of a particular tenant. Even if most of an estate was held on non-manorial tenures, court rolls may still be a valuable source for the history of a few tenements which remained copyhold, possibly over a period of two or three centuries.

Manor court records, like those of all courts, were kept in Latin until 1734 but later material should present no more problems than any other type of deed. Another technical problem which affects many early modern sources besides deeds is the practice of dating documents according to 'regnal years' rather than the ordinary calendar, e.g. 2 March, 12 Geo. III, meaning 1772. There are two standard technical manuals for this and other problems of chronology (by C. R. Cheney, and by Powicke and Fryde), such as the practice in medieval deeds of dating events according to saints' days. This virtually died out at the Reformation in England, except for the survival of Lady Day (25 March) and Michaelmas (29 September) as favoured dates for the execution of deeds or payment of rent. Another point to remember is that until 1752 New Year's Day was reckoned to be 25 March rather 1 January, which affects dating (according to modern usage) of documents in most of the first three months of the year.

Before listing deeds fully, archivists usually arrange them according to the property (or at least parish) to which they relate; if the collection has arrived at the office intact, it will often consist of bundles, one for each property. Within each bundle, deeds will usually be arranged chronologically, so that one can trace a succession of owners. If you are looking at deeds not in a record office (for example the deeds to your own house at the bank or building society) which have not been listed by an archivist, they will be easier to understand if you look at them in date order. Apart from anything else, it may become obvious from a series of deeds arranged in this way that the description of the property was copied from one deed to another without revision. Thus, 'all that newly erected messuage, tenement or dwelling house' (i.e. just a house) mentioned in 1850 may actually have been built in 1800, when the same phrase also occurs, but for the first time. Interesting details such as 'now wholly or partly occupied by an iron furnace lately erected thereon' may be copied into deeds postdating the demolition of the works; 'abutting westwardly on the lands of the Abbot of Welbeck' may occur in a deed of 1700 and be obviously wrong, but is useful evidence for the pre-1539 history of a neighbouring property.

The description of urban property in deeds before recent times is usually too imprecise to identify unless the deed is part of a bundle known to relate to a specific modern address: 'all that messuage . . . in a road called St Mary's Gate' will only become 'all that property known as No 22 St Mary's Gate' about 1900 and if the older deeds have become separated from modern conveyances it is very difficult to re-unite them. In rural areas, named farms can normally be identified, especially in upland districts where a name applied to a single homestead rather than a hamlet or village. Deeds merely conveying fields can sometimes be matched up with references to field-names on nineteenth-century maps.

There is one final short-cut to tracing the history of property from deeds which may help those put off by the size of the documents and the legal verbiage. On most bundles that are still intact there should be an 'Abstract of Title', drawn up by the vendor's solicitor when the property changed hands, to show the purchaser that the vendor was entitled to sell the estate. Sometimes the abstract mentions deeds now lost; generally it will provide an adequate summary of each of the existing deeds. This is often worth having photocopied, because the abstract of each deed will be so concise as not to allow for much further shortening, whereas post-1700 original deeds are hardly ever worth having copied. They are usually too big to go on small copiers and so have to be done in several sheets; after you have stuck these together you will find you have merely paid to have a great deal of common form copied. It is sometimes useful to have plans found on Victorian deeds copied, unless you merely make a note of the field-numbers and relate them to an Ordnance Survey or tithe map.

If you are trying to trace the history of an individual property, for example your own house or an ironworks or a cornmill, estate records, deeds and the maps described in the next chapter are the most useful sources for identifying specific properties and their owners or occupiers. They are also basic to a general study of landownership in a particular parish, whether it was a wholly rural community or a parish which became a suburb or a mining village or a factory town, in the nineteenth century or more recently. One or two other sources, which may be helpful in some cases, may also be mentioned here.

Between 1780 and 1832 the clerk of the peace in each county kept land tax assessments—duplicates of the lists of people paying land tax in each parish, because only those who paid above a certain level were eligible to vote in parliamentary elections. Land tax was levied annually between 1692 and 1949 but for most of that period all that survives (in the Public Record Office) are returns of the amount paid by each parish, not each person. For this one important fifty-year period, however, during which there were major shifts in land-ownership in much of England and Wales as a result of agricultural and industrial change, detailed records are available locally for each county. In principle, land tax assessments list for each parish for every year the owners and occupiers of all the land and the amount of tax they paid thereon. In practice, there are a number of complications on which a rather technical literature has been written, but for most local historians land tax assessments are a very useful guide to 'who was who' in their parish between 1780 and 1832. They are especially valuable when there are no estate records, since they at least show who were the main landowners in this period, even if it is impossible exactly to relate the amount of tax paid to acreage owned or occupied. Very small occupiers often do not appear in the assessments or may be embraced under the 'Mr Smith and Others' which will sometimes appear in the occupiers' column, but for all but the smallest owners and for the larger tenant farmers they are a useful source.

Identifying individual houses in land tax assessments is not easy even after the introduction of a column listing the 'premises' on which tax was paid, although in a small village where you know who was living at a particular house in, say, 1790, you may be able to follow its history through to 1830 by checking when the name changes in the list (the assessment being written out in the same order year after year). In towns this is usually impossible, as it is in any parish when little or no detail was entered in the premises column. Industrial buildings or houses of particular importance may be itemised from the start; for the cotton industry of the East Midlands, where many small concerns had a fleeting, otherwise undocumented existence in the 1780s and 1790s land tax assessments have been used to establish dates between which mills were in operation and by whom they were worked.

Local rates, again mainly for the second half of the eighteenth century and for the early nineteenth century, sometimes leave records (*ratebooks*) which may be used in much the same way as land tax assessments. They will usually be found in parish collections and typically consist of lists of people and the amount of rate paid (whatever rate it was). If there is no topographical detail at all in the list there is little hope of establishing more than the fact that John Smith was paying poor rate that year; if he is described as 'John Smith, for Townend Farm' that is more helpful. In towns where the ratebook was compiled by street and you can establish independently the names of one or two contemporary occupiers, you may be able to work out that the list is arranged systematically, starting at one end of the road and going along each side in turn, in which case you may be able to assign each ratepayer to a house with some confidence. If you have a series of ratebooks for a town, going as late as an early census year (1841 or 1851) for which you can work out house-by-house occupancy from the enumerator's book, a close study of each book working backwards may enable you to trace changes of occupancy back, say, to about 1800. Some local historians have tried to do this starting from the tithe map of 1840 and going from there to the last land tax assessment (1832), then going back year by year to 1780. This is very time consuming for a place of any size, needing group effort if possible, and its success depends on relative stability in the layout of a town, lack of change in the 1830s, and having a detailed tithe award in which occupiers are listed in full, rather than with the 'Self and Others' formula often used in built-up areas.

For the later nineteenth century ratebooks become so bulky, and so much of the information derived from them about individuals is available elsewhere, that many local record offices only keep a sample of each parish—usually for census years (1841, 1851, etc) so that they can be used in conjunction with the enumerators' books (p. 34) to locate individuals and particular houses. More generally, ratebooks of this period are one source (the other main one being Ordnance Survey maps, see pp. 72–7) through which the growth of suburbs and new streets in expanding towns, may be traced by checking a succession of books in order to pick up the first appearance of a street or estate.

People

The previous section explained what sources in a local record office are likely to be most useful in tracing the history of landownership or the history of a single house. The same documents, of course, like those created by local administration, also mention people, and anyone trying to trace a particular family or individual will find most of them useful for this purpose as well. In an office which has had the chance to list and index its deposited collections in depth, and possibly some of its official and diocesan material also, a search of the personal name index for a particular person or family is always worthwhile and takes virtually no time. What does take time, and beyond a certain point is not usually worth the effort, is searching large, unlisted or unindexed collections on the off-chance of finding a reference to the person you are interested in. On the other hand, record offices contain a number of important classes of material specifically concerned with individuals which, while not often indexed by name, are worth searching either for a genealogical project or some more general enquiry. Here it is worth reflecting on the fact that almost all local history, from the most mindless ancestor-hunting to the thorough study of a community, is concerned to some extent with people, as indeed are most local records. A bundle of deeds does not really tell you the 'history of your house', since most houses have no 'history' as such: it supplies the names of the people who owned and occupied that house. Similarly, nineteenth-century business records or the minute-books of local authorities become much more interesting when you look behind the letter-books and resolutions at who was writing the letters or passing the resolutions. All local historians, not just genealogists, should know how to trace people in the past.

The basic sources for this sort of research are so well known from their use by genealogists as not to need detailed explanation here. Thus *parish registers* (and the 'bishops' transcripts' made of them each year for the archdeacon's visitation) are usually the best place in which to start looking for someone between about 1550 and 1830, once you know which parish he lived in, or at least roughly where. Before the middle of the sixteenth century you are much more heavily dependent on the records of central government (Chapter 5) or records created by the ownership of land; the latter of course remain useful down to modern times.

The other standard genealogical source long used in conjunction with parish registers is *wills*, plus more recently, the *inventories* of the deceased's personal estate (but not his freehold property) filed with a will. Until 1858 probate of wills (and the formal 'administration' of intestate estates where the next of kin did not simply divide things up between them) came within the jurisdiction of the church courts, whose records are now mostly in county record offices. Because of the demand for them by genealogists they are usually fairly well indexed by person, less well by place and often not at all by occupation. A similar demand has ensured that accurate, up-to-date guides are available to probate material. The lowest church official who had probate jurisdiction was normally the archdeacon, in whose court wills of people with property in a single place would generally be proved. Somewhat larger estates still confined to a single diocese would be dealt with in the bishop's court; in most of Wales and in some English dioceses wills were all proved in the diocesan rather than archdeaconry court. Finally, there was the prerogative jurisdiction of the two archbishops of York and Canterbury (of whom the latter had ultimate jurisdiction over the whole country), in whose courts were proved the wills of people with property in more than one diocese or those which were likely to prove contentious. The records of the Prerogative Court of York are in the custody of the Borthwick Institute of Historical Research of York University; those of the Prerogative Court of Canterbury are in the Public Record Office (p. 137). Other pre-1858 probate records are held locally, including most of those for the various oddities in the system ('peculiars') which existed before 1858. Welsh church records, including probate material, are all at the National Library at Aberystwyth.

Once you have established which local court people from your village, or the family in which you are interested, would have dealt with in probate matters, it is usually fairly simple to check whether a particular person left a will, or if letters of administration were taken out for his estate. Wills, as genealogical textbooks have long told us, are invaluable in supplying the names of the children, nephews, nieces and so on of the testator and thus fitting together what may be unconnected references in the parish register. They are also much more personal in character than deeds or administrative records. If the original will taken to court by the executor has survived, it will also give an indication, from the quality of the handwriting and the presence or absence of a signature or 'mark', as to the literacy of the writer; alternatively, there may only be a copy of the will written into a contemporary will register, where the name at the end is not an autograph.

From the early sixteenth century to the early eighteenth, it was customary for an inventory to be made of the personal estate of anyone whose affairs came before the probate court, and for this to be 'exhibited' (not proved) by the executors when they presented the will for probate, or by administrators when they sought letters of administration. During the last thirty years these documents, which for most parts of the country survive in great number, have become well known and many have been published. Because they are inventories of personal, not real, estate, they are not a complete measure of the deceased's wealth, but where they have been compiled room by room they give a fascinating picture of how someone's house was furnished, and the total valuation is obviously a rough guide to wealth and social standing. In rural communities few sources are so useful for the history of farming, as opposed to landownership, since detailed inventories will itemise crops, animals and implements. For the history of early modern towns, inventories are a basic source for establishing how people earned a living and what sort of capital was needed in different trades. Lists of creditors and debtors in both rural and urban inventories reveal how much small-scale money-lending went on in this period, and from what sort of area tradesmen bought raw materials or sold finished goods.

If you are interested in a specific person or family from the sixteenth century onwards (comparatively few medieval wills survive and no probate inventories in the later sense) check to see whether a will survives. Most people did not make wills and most families did not bother with the expense of taking out letters of administration, but where there is a will it will certainly be worth looking at (with any supporting documents such as an inventory) and probably having copied. The handwriting of pre-1660 original wills (and most registered copies) is usually fairly difficult for the beginner but this is one source where the effort to read the hand is likely to be rewarded.

Probate records are equally valuable for the local historian studying a community as a whole. Especially in parishes which have no surviving estate material, wills and inventories will often be the largest single source of information on the community before 1800. In a county where the wills have been indexed by place it is easy enough to find all the documents for your parish; where you have to search an unprinted name index looking for references to a parish it will take much longer to identify all the relevant material. Even in this case, however, the value of probate records is such that it is worthwhile; it is also worth looking at all the documents filed for each testator. It is not the case that wills are useful for genealogists and inventories for local historians; this is a bogus distinction. For a detailed community study it is even worth going through the largely formal bonds surviving from grants of letters of administration to the next of kin of men who died without leaving wills, since odd snippets of information about individuals will appear here which may not elsewhere.

In 1858 probate jurisdiction was transferred to a lay court which established a network of district registries not dissimilar from the diocesan courts which they replaced, as well as a principal registry in London, whose records are now at Somerset House. A major change, however, was that instead of each court keeping its own index to grants, a printed calendar was compiled annually for the whole of England and Wales, listing in one sequence all the wills provided, and in another all the grants of administration, irrespective of where the transaction took place. This greatly simplifies the process of tracing a grant, especially since the index volumes from 1858 to 1928 have now been moved from district registries to record offices. They can also be consulted at Somerset House and copies of the wills obtained either from there or, in those districts where the relevant will registers have been transferred, from the county record office. Civil wills, and indeed most wills after 1750, do not have inventories with them.

In the same way that probate jurisdiction was overhauled so, somewhat earlier in the nineteenth century, was the *registration* of 'vital' events (births, marriages and deaths). In 1837 the compulsory registration of birth and death was introduced in England and Wales, a far more thorough system that was ever achieved by relying on the registration of baptism and burial by the churches. In the case of marriage registration, the Church of England and to a lesser extent the other denominations were taken into partnership with the state, so that all marriages were recorded in civil registers, kept either by the registrar or incumbent, and a duplicate record was kept of church weddings. This system of registration has not changed very much since 1837 and its working is well known. The Registrar General's headquarters are in London (St Catherine's House, Strand, London WC2), with a network of district registrars throughout the country. There are national indexes at St Catherine's House but searches can also be made in the district where the event is believed to have taken place. Information from registration certificates can only be supplied in the form of very expensive copy certificates, although with uncommon names and imaginative use of the St Catherine's House indexes the need to obtain certificates can be kept to a minimum.

Birth, marriage and death certificates, like post-1858 wills, are not merely the staple fare of genealogists; they can be useful for more general enquiries. The history of a house, an estate or a business may turn on family relationships as revealed by a comparatively modern will or marriage. It is unusual for a genealogist not to be able to trace a moderately well-off family back to about 1800, through vital registration certificates and probate grants, and the same process in reverse is sometimes worth pursuing (for rather different motives) by a local historian. Not all family, business and estate papers are in record offices and libraries, and if you are interested in, say, a small estate wound up about 1920, or a business that closed in the 1950s, it may be worth tracing the present whereabouts of the family concerned, using ordinary genealogical sources (plus such obvious material as the telephone directory, *Who's Who* and electors' lists), to ask if anything survives in their possession. If documents do turn up, it is then best to ask the local record office to try to secure them on deposit or take copies, rather than make an offer to the owner yourself.

So far this section has been concerned with tracing people in general in archival sources, who can of course often be found also in printed material in libraries. One other source of this kind which is often available in county record offices and, for more recent periods, in local libraries, is *registers of electors* for each borough and county from 1832 to the present. Before 1867, and in country districts until 1884, the franchise remained restricted to men of a certain wealth; thus, nineteenth-century electoral registers are not a complete list of residents, but they are nonetheless very useful in locating individuals once one knows roughly where they were living at a particular time. They are not alphabetical lists but are arranged topographically, so that a complete search of a large town for one person is a lengthy undertaking; conversely, once full addresses for urban properties emerged, it is easy enough to establish who was living at a particular house in a given year, and in country parishes with individually named farms possible at an earlier period.

County record offices also contain several classes of material which are useful for tracing individuals engaged in specific activities, particularly *criminal* or socially undesirable ones such as being poor. Today, most criminal offences are tried before magistrates in courts that are the successors to petty sessions, which were so called to distinguish them from the grander courts of quarter sessions, meetings of (in theory) all the magistrates for a county or large borough. Modern magistrates' court records less than 30 years old are not available for inspection and those of petty sessions are not well preserved, since the proceedings, before one or two magistrates resident in a locality, were relatively informal. The criminal records of quarter sessions, however, are for most counties reasonably complete from 1800 if not earlier; they are a good source for the history of crime which was too serious to be dealt with in petty sessions but which did not on the other hand reach the assize courts in England (whose records are in the PRO) or the court of great sessions in Wales (whose records are at the National Library). As well as providing the raw material for general studies of crime in the localities, quarter sessions material can be used by local historians interested in a particular place who are prepared to search fairly voluminous material for references to their own locality. This is obviously more likely to yield results in a town, as opposed to a village where a local magistrate kept order and hardly any matters went to quarter sessions.

Although *the poor* undoubtedly leave less behind them in the past than the rich, one well known local source for their study is the examinations and removal orders executed by magistrates enforcing the pre-1834 poor law, assisted by the overseers of the poor in each parish. If the overseers encountered a stranger who might become a charge on the parish because of age, poverty, pregnancy or infirmity they normally presented him or her to the nearest magistrate. The magistrate would then extract from the stranger the name of their home parish, or at least a place where they had previously lived long enough to gain legal 'settlement' and entitlement to poor relief. If they could not prove that they were entitled to legal settlement in the place into which they had come, the magistrate would sign a removal order addressed to the overseers: this allowed them to convey the unfortunate victim to the first parish along the road towards that in which they had settlement, however far that might be. The removal orders may have ended up either in quarter sessions records or with the overseers' accounts in parish collections; examinations are usually in the latter. They do not survive for all parishes, and some places—for example villages in the Midlands standing astride Watling Street or some other major highway—will have more than a remote parish in the West Country, but some record offices have compiled a consolidated index of personal and place-names for settlement papers, however these may have reached the office. Like quarter sessions material, this source can be used to study poverty in a particular county, to trace ancestors who fell on hard times, or to add to the overall picture of life in your village in the seventeenth and eighteenth centuries. Removal orders are largely formal, but examinations contain much human detail of movement from place to place in search of work.

Industry and transport

A number of printed sources for the local history of industry and transport, especially nineteenth-century directories, were mentioned in Chapter 2; this is also an area well served by secondary material, either the voluminous literature of railway history, the rather newer but now fairly extensive bibliography of canal history, the books on road transport and road vehicles, and the vast quantity of books, pamphlets and trails which marked the rise of industrial archaeology in the 1960s. The local historian interested either in transport generally in his parish, or in local industry, should be able to find a fair amount of information from such material. Archival sources available locally, or indeed anywhere, especially for small scale industry or minor transport undertakings, may be more limited.

If you wish to pursue the history of a particular firm, or an industry made up of several businesses, the best way to start is almost always to compile lists of names from each available nineteenth-century directory (p. 30). If it is an industry carried out in fairly extensive premises which can be identified on large-scale maps (Chapter 4) each of the firms can then be located on the ground, where buildings may survive. Workshop or cottage industries, such as nailmaking or stocking knitting, are obviously harder to trace in this way. Industries with a strongly 'territorial' character, such as coal-mining or iron and steel manufacture, should certainly be studied topographically, together with associated railways, tramways or branch canals, and industrial housing. Once you have worked out the dates between which a business operated, or located on the ground the site of an ironworks, water-mill or whatever, it is worth turning to the resources of a local record office.

Since only in a few cases will business records survive, it is best to think of how else one can reconstruct the history of a works or mill. Several pieces of relevant advice have been offered on earlier pages: identify the parish in which the enterprise operated and see what is available generally in the way of unprinted maps or estate records, the latter possibly including leases by a ground landlord whose muniments have survived where his lessees' business papers have not (p. 54); search land tax assessments (p. 59) to try to establish the dates between which, for example, an ironworks is mentioned, and note the occupiers' names; check the personal names index for all the names you have culled from directories in case stray deeds, including partnership deeds, have come into the office from solicitors; try the main genealogical sources (the census, parish registers and wills) to build up biographical details of the owners of the mill or colliery you are interested in. The approach to avoid is that of merely asking the archivist for any business papers from the firm of Bloggs & Co, dyers and bleachers of No Mans Heath, 1860–1900, since you will almost certainly be told, on the basis of a brief search of the indexes, that there are none in the office. What there will be, however, will be maps marking Messrs Bloggs's premises, which may perhaps have been converted from an earlier water corn-mill belonging to a local estate, whose muniments may include a bundle of deeds listed merely as 'No Mans Heath Mill, leases, 1750–1860'. These might trace half a dozen previous occupiers of the site and possibly mention other industries which used the mill before it became a bleachworks. If the last directory to name the works identifies the owners as Bloggs & Jones, try the record office index under the other name. Possibly Mr Jones's solicitor, who wound up the business when Bloggs died, has deposited material which includes probate or bankruptcy papers. None of this comes under the heading of 'business records' but it is far more typical of what is to be found for most companies in a record office than is sometimes suggested in textbooks. Few eighteenth- or nineteenth-century business enterprises of any size have not left some trace in local records, but equally, for even fewer will the office have any but fragmentary company archives proper.

If a local historian is fortunate, he will find that perhaps for one business in the town a good set of records has been deposited, or more commonly rescued by an alert archivist. Apart from deeds, which may include both conveyances of the premises occupied by the firm and deeds establishing or dissolving the formal co-partnership through which most companies operated before modern limited liability became general, accounting records are probably the most likely to have survived. There may be a run of sales ledgers, with an account for each customer, in which hopefully goods will have been entered as '200 tramplates, 45 lb per yard, marked "G. U. CANAL COY" ', not merely as 'Goods'. Or there may be a partnership ledger, setting out how the original share capital was raised, what dividends were paid, what was done when the first partners died, and how the nominal value of the firm grew. The other most common survival tends to be correspondence, either letters received by the firm or copies of out-letters. Whether loose, in bundles or in letter-books the most interesting of these will probably be enquiries about products or estimates supplied to prospective customers. In a large collection a great many of the out-letters may prove on examination to be chasing unpaid accounts or dealing with other routine matters.

The archive material for two of the major nineteenth-century industrial staples in which local historians are often interested should perhaps be mentioned separately. Early *colliery* records, up to about the middle of the nineteenth century, are scarce outside the North Eastern coalfield, which was in this period by far the largest producer. Elsewhere the typical unit of production was too small to generate much in the way of records, and maps and leases surviving in estate collections are often the only sources. More modern company records were vested in the National Coal Board in 1947 and are legally public records, although they are in local custody. While some series of partners' and directors' minutes, sales ledgers and letter-books have become available in this way, the bulk of NCB transfers to county record offices generally outweighs their value for the local history of the industry. Much of the material is turn-of-the-century or later and for many pits there are only such subsidiary records as signing-on books (listing men as they joined the colliery) rather than basic administrative or accounting records. A great deal was destroyed by the private owners on the eve of nationalisation, as folk-memory in every coalfield will testify. For the *iron industry*, there are several major collections for the eighteenth century preserved among the muniments of families who controlled the large partnerships which dominated the industry in this period, and some earlier material, especially for the Weald and parts of the West Midlands. For the Industrial Revolution, however, and the rest of the nineteenth century when, at least to begin with, the typical company was a small concern with only one works, far fewer business records survive, except perhaps deeds, and most have been used for published company histories. Later material, especially post-1870 records of the steel industry, has generally passed into the hands of the British Steel Corporation, who maintain an archive service of their own, rather than the county record offices.

If two major industries such as coal and iron are poorly documented in the nineteenth century, it may be appreciated how little can usually be found for the typical local business. Approaches to existing old-established firms direct are often unproductive, unless one already has some personal contact. Either the letter is not answered or the company say that nothing has survived. This may be the case, or some long-serving official in the company secretary's office is guarding material for his forthcoming centenary history and doesn't want anyone else to look at it.

The archives of local *retailing* are normally non-existent, and anyone interested in tracing the history of shopping will usually be dependent on directories, old newspapers and the like, which together can produce quite a full account of the period after about 1830. For a much earlier period, urban inventories often include a handful of good examples relating to shopkeepers, especially mercers and drapers, which tend to be selected for publication. Directories are usually the only source available for the local history of carrying and coach services; they are also a good starting-point for a perennially popular project: tracing the history of *inns* in a town. For the fifty years or so prior to the start of detailed local directories it is worth looking at 'alehouse recognisances', a category of quarter sessions record, which supply the names of licensees and those who stood surety for them for good behaviour to the licensing justices each year. By the 1810s or 1820s the name of the pub is sometimes also given. Again, for the earlier history of inns, probate inventories of the seventeenth century are an unrivalled source, although the pubs are rarely named.

For the history of *roads* themselves, there are several sources in a local record office, although these have often been pretty thoroughly worked over and it may be possible to rely on secondary material. Today, most roads are maintained by county councils, whose responsibility in this field dates from 1889, when it was handed over by the justices. Quarter sessions exercised mainly a supervisory role in the earlier period, the actual maintenance of roads being the job, usually ill-executed, of the parish surveyors until 1835, thereafter of district highway boards. From the early eighteenth century until the middle of the nineteenth many main roads were taken out of the hands of the parish and maintained by turnpike trusts, who, under the authority of a local Act of Parliament, repaired and sometimes built stretches of road, borrowed money to do so, and attempted to repay the money by charging tolls for the use of the improved roads. Turnpike trust records may include, as well as the printed Act of Parliament setting up the body, minutes of a managing committee and accounts. Either may supply the date of construction, and possibly the name of an architect, of a surviving tollhouse. Similar information about bridges should be sought in quarter sessions records, which may contain a separate group of papers for the county surveyor or orders by the justices (in the order books) to have 'county bridges' (i.e. those on main roads for which the county and not the parish took responsibility) built, rebuilt or repaired. If your village stands on a main road carried over a river on a fine eighteenth-century bridge, the chances are that its construction will be mentioned in quarter sessions records.

The improvement of *river navigation* between about 1660 and 1760 took much the same institutional form as the turnpiking of roads, with a body of commissioners acting under authority of a local Act. When *canals* were built in the later eighteenth century or early nineteenth somewhat different Acts were obtained incorporating shareholders into a company which owned the canal and associated works outright. This type of corporation was also adopted by the promoters of the more ambitious pre-locomotive *railway* schemes of the period 1800–30, and subsequently followed by the early main line railway companies of the next fifteen years, which evolved into the large national concerns of the later nineteenth century. When the railways, most of the canals and the larger docks were brought into public ownership after the second world war, the British Transport Commission set up a record office to house its archives centrally. This material is now in the hands of the Public Record Office at

Kew, who have changed all the mnemonic references one used to be able to follow quite simply (such as GW for the records of the Great Western Railway) to meaningless numbers prefaced by the equally unhelpful group letters RAIL. As a result all the footnotes in dozens of books published by David & Charles in the 1960s and 1970s have become obsolete. Thanks to the energy of this firm and its authors, however, the railway and canal companies' history is now fairly well known, and for any transport undertaking of this period there will probably be a published history of some kind.

Since almost all railway and most waterway records are held centrally this leaves comparatively little scope for the local historian without ready access to Kew. The one source for transport history that can be found in a local record office, although it also has uses outside this field, is the plan deposited with the clerk of the peace in advance of application to parliament for authority to build a canal or railway, whether or not the scheme was proceeded with (p. 89). The more modern history of road transport has a somewhat smaller enthusiasts' following than railways, but for anyone interested in the tram, trolleybus or motor-bus undertakings of local authorities there should normally be minutes of the appropriate committee among the council's records. Business records of the numerous private operators who flourished briefly between the wars are very scarce.

This chapter is the longest in the book and has tried to summarise what is available (or not) in most county record offices for some of the topics most often pursued or asked about by amateur local historians. It does not provide a comprehensive guide to the contents of local offices or go into as much detail as more specialised textbooks. Nor has it tried to rival genealogical manuals in its advice on records used mainly by family historians, although I have tried to suggest that much of this material has a wider value. The reader with a general interest in his (preferably fairly small) community should find something of value in each section of the chapter; those who merely want to trace the history of the brickworks at the end of their garden may pick up some hints but will soon have to turn to books specifically concerned with brickmaking. However wide or narrow your research project, one thing is certain: that in addition to using the printed sources outlined in the previous chapter and the archive material described here, you will also wish to use maps, both new and old, and indeed may well have started by looking at whatever you are interested in on a map. Since they are so basic to local history and are to be found in both libraries and record offices a separate chapter has been allotted to them, which amplifies the passing references in this and the previous chapter.

Chapter Four
MAPS

All introductory books dwell heavily on the importance of maps for local history, both those published by the Ordnance Survey and earlier unprinted maps, especially those drawn up for tithe or enclosure awards. This is usually coupled with a similar stress on the landscape itself, as portrayed in maps and visible on the ground. There is a long tradition of interest among English antiquaries in the value of field evidence, which was one of the aspects of the subject urged most strongly by the Leicester School, especially Hoskins himself, in the post-war renaissance of local history. Most amateurs who become interested in local history need little reminder of the value of landscape evidence, since they tend to be the sort of people who already go for walks in the country, visit historic houses and join the National Trust. Furthermore, the first sources many local historians look at are maps, particularly those fairly readily available in public libraries. This chapter has the twin aims of setting out what map sources are available, either for the whole country or particular parishes, and how they can be used to recreate past landscapes. The chapter following considers the use of physical evidence itself, whether from archaeological excavation, fieldwork or the surveying of old buildings.

Ordnance Survey maps

Great Britain has the good fortune to be the best mapped country in the world, thanks to the work of the world's finest mapmaking organisation, the Ordnance Survey. All local historians will be familiar with its best known publication, the 1:50,000 map of the whole country, which has replaced the earlier one-inch survey. Useful though the sheets of the 1:50,000 survey are for coverage of a fairly large region, an essential investment for the local historian interested in a small area are the relevant sheets of the 2½ inch map (1:25,000). This was first issued shortly after the war in a provisional edition, using pre-war material, to provide a new intermediate scale between the one-inch series and the larger scales. It has now been re-issued for the whole country in a second edition, with better use of colour and drawing on recent survey data. Although it does not help greatly with the field-study of particular sites, it is extremely useful as a portable folding map on a scale on which it is possible to mark field boundaries as well as buildings, roads, railways and natural features.

The original 2½ inch map was produced by reducing older sheets of what was then the six-inch survey (1:10,560), which has now been rescaled as 1:10,000. This is published for all but the most remote parts of the country and, together with its larger brother, the 25 inch plan (which has in fact always been published on the slightly smaller scale of 1:2500), is the OS map with the longest history after the one-inch survey.

The Ordnance Survey was established in the 1790s to prepare up-to-date maps of the three maritime counties of south-east England —Kent, Surrey and Sussex—as a preparation for repelling possible French invaders. After the war ended in 1815 the survey work of the Board of Ordnance was continued and gradually extended to the rest of the country. The original maps were published on a scale which had already become common in the eighteenth century for county maps (see p. 92), one inch to the mile, although the OS sheets formed a continuous set for the whole country, unlike their privately produced predecessors. The 'Old Series' of the one-inch map was not completed until about 1870, by which date many sheets had become badly out of date as towns expanded, railways were built and the English landscape changed more drastically than it had for centuries. No systematic revision was carried out on the old series (for which the name 'First Edition' implies a neatness in publication which was not the case), apart from the addition of railway lines as they were built (the OS did not fall into the trap of some private mapmakers of inserting projected railways, many of which were never built). Even after railways were added, however, sheets continued to be issued bearing the original date of publication and there is virtually no way of establishing exactly when a revision was issued, or how much other detail was changed apart from the railways.

Most local libraries and record offices have copies of the old series one-inch map for their area. Especially where the sheets have been trimmed and mounted, thus removing any dates at all, it is difficult to discover when the sheet was surveyed, particularly if it was one of those where there was a long delay between survey and publication. Some years ago David & Charles produced facsimile reprints of the old series maps for the whole country, folded in the same way as a modern one-inch map. These have some value in making the maps available again in a convenient format, but the standard of repro-duction was low and the sheets used for the new edition varied wildly over the period in which the old series was published. In some cases, composite maps were made up from the quarter-sheets in which certain areas were originally published; where different quarters are from different printings the new edition may have railway lines stopping half-way across the sheet. J. B. Harley's marginal commentary on each of the reprints explains some of these difficulties, but the project fell short of a scholarly facsimile edition. Harry Margary (Lympne Castle, Kent) is now publishing a series closer to this ideal but the maps are being issued in volumes and are much more expensive. The underlying problem with any scheme of this kind is that there is no complete set of what can properly be called a 'first edition' of the one-inch map. The Ordnance Survey's own archives suffered badly in the war and neither the British Museum nor the Bodleian has complete holdings (Cambridge University and the other national libraries did not then have a copyright privilege which extended to maps).

The old series one-inch maps are of some use for the study of local topography, coming mid-way between the privately produced maps of the late eighteenth century and the second edition of the OS, but the scale is too small to do more than identify the existence or non-existence of certain fairly obvious features. Tracing tramroads in mining areas is a good example of a project for which the old series OS can be useful; the gradual spread of suburbs over the period 1830–60 is a subject on which they are highly unreliable. The local historian making a detailed study of his parish will probably wish to supplement a photocopy of the first one-inch map with a copy of the earlier drawing from which it was engraved, which is on a scale of two inches to the mile and may contain details suppressed on the published map (Fig. 3, p. 102). The original drawings were lost in the war but photostats had previously been made for the British Museum, whose Map Room can supply copies; for Wales there is a set of photostats at the National Library.

By the middle of the nineteenth century it was clear that the work of the Ordnance Survey needed overhauling. The department had already done some surveying intended for publication on a much larger scale than 1:63,360, for example in Ireland and the West Riding, and in the 1870s began the publication, following closely on survey in most areas, of a completely new 'second edition', which marks the beginning of modern OS publishing. A policy of concentrating on three scales was established, which has lasted to the present. The *one-inch* map was issued in folding sheets with some use of colour, and thus became popular with the growing numbers who wished to explore the countryside on foot or, later, bicycle, an activity which became easier as the network of railway branch-lines was extended. For those who wanted a larger scale, which included some ordinary purchasers but mainly meant landowners, local authorities and public utilities, the survey was published at what then seemed a logical scale of *six inches* to the mile, except in mountainous districts. Finally, for those who needed a large-scale plan of built-up areas, a *25 inch* plan was produced.

While the second (and later) editions of the one-inch map are of little interest to local historians, the publication of the first six-inch and 25 inch maps marks the beginning of the period in which one can trace the micro-topography of almost anywhere. Both the larger scales are useful in different ways. If you are interested in a particular feature, such as a country house, cottonmill, colliery, ironworks or railway station, the 25 inch plans are indispensable (Fig. 8, p. 107). They are sufficiently large to mark standard gauge railway lines to a scale width (which the smaller maps do not) and show not merely the existence but the shape of most buildings. At an ironworks you can count the number of blast furnaces; at a country house you can see if the conservatory was there. Boundaries of fields and other parcels of land are shown, with the acreage given for all but small private house-plots. Because of their aesthetic as well as cartographic appeal, the first edition 25 inch plans are a marvellous source for bringing alive the landscape of the 1870s.

The first edition of the six inch map, although obviously less detailed than the 25 inch plans and visually less appealing, nonetheless has its uses (Figs. 5 and 7, pp. 104 and 106). For one thing, a single photocopy from a six-inch sheet may well cover a whole parish, which will not be the case with the larger plans. Secondly, if you are interested in the evolution of a complete landscape, such as a parish, a copy from the six-inch map gives you an overall picture of the extent of building, the existence of parks and woodland, industrial features and so on, which small extracts from the 25 inch plan do not. Thirdly, the six-inch map is usually a better base on which to mark up earlier features, for example from the tithe map (p. 77), than the 25 inch plan, unless you are concerned with a very small area.

Whether you are interested in a whole landscape or only one feature therein, an obvious step in any topographical project is to get a photocopy of each six-inch or 25 inch map from 1880 to the present day. There was an initial revision of the two larger scales about 1900 and another between the wars; since 1945, for most of which time the OS have been working to bring their primary survey back up to date after inter-war neglect, there has been a process of continuous revision of the large scales, so that there will probably be a couple of issues of each map for your area, the more recent six-inch sheet having the National Grid superimposed. The grid should be familiar to users from the small scale maps and for the larger scales forms a reference system to the sheets, which are identified by the 10 km. or 1 km. square which they cover. The older large scale sheets were numbered separately within each county in the case of the six-inch survey, while each 25 inch plan, which covered one-sixteenth of the area of a six-inch map, was given a number derived from the six-inch sheet number. Thus, Glamorganshire XXI was the reference for a six-inch sheet in the County Series, within which the 25 inch plan of the NE corner of the area would be Glamorganshire XXI.4.

Crown copyright in Ordnance Survey maps lasts for fifty years from the date of publication, after which they may be copied freely. To supply copies of more recent maps, a library or record office must have a licence from the Ordnance Survey, whose copyright branch operates with a ferocity, shared only by the Performing Rights Society, which makes unauthorised copying of current maps distinctly unwise. The Ordnance Survey themselves now mostly sell the large scale plans as photocopies made from 35 mm. negative material supplied to trade agents. These are much cheaper than conventionally printed plans and allow for the quicker publication of new survey data, although they do not look as nice as earlier editions. A technical rather than legal problem in copying old OS maps is that on small office copiers it is possible to tear fragile sheet maps, which has made some libraries and record offices reluctant to make cheap copies. The staff may insist that they can only supply copies made photographically at considerable expense by a commercial plan-copying firm, or they may have access to in-house copying facilities in the county surveyor's department. This is one instance where access to source material has actually become more difficult in the last ten years, as custodians of material have become concerned about the survival of their map collections. The greater use of 35 mm. or larger negatives and large format microprinters for older as well as current OS maps is probably one long-term answer. A simpler solution is to rely on tracing extracts from maps, which is normally still permitted in libraries and record offices, as long as a clear plastic sheet is inserted between the map and tracing paper or film.

For a local historian working on a rural landscape, or a coalfield area, a sequence of six-inch or 25 inch maps will give a clear picture of how the area has changed in the last century. If you are working on a town or looking at the growth of suburbs there are some other Ordnance Survey plans that provide an even fuller picture of the developing townscape. One of these is the current 50 inch (1:1250) survey of built-up areas, of which each sheet covers a quarter of the area of a 25 inch plan. This was introduced after the war to provide a better base in towns where the 25 inch plan had become congested. There are no older editions on this scale, except a one-off set of plans produced for the Inland Revenue at the turn of the century in connection with a revaluation for rating, which is merely a mechanical enlargement of the then 25 inch sheets with no additional detail. The Ordnance Survey no longer publish plans on a scale larger than 1:1250, but most local authorities produce their own 1:500 scale sheets for particular purposes, which is simple enough to do with modern scale-changing equipment and legal for OS licensees. A local historian working in detail on urban topograpy may find it useful to get hold of a plan on this scale from a sympathetic borough surveyor.

In the 1870s, as part of the second edition survey, the OS produced a magnificent series of town plans, mostly on the 'ten foot scale' (1:500), which are perhaps the finest maps they have ever published (Fig. 9, p. 108). For anyone interested in a town covered on this scale they are invaluable, coming just before slum clearance and road-building started in most places. Not merely is every parcel boundary and every house shown, but for public buildings there are interior plans and the seating capacity; street furniture is shown to scale, and there is far more narrative than on the 25 inch sheets. Railway installations are also shown in great detail. This exercise has never been repeated, but a generation earlier the OS were engaged by the newly established Board of Health to produce surveys for towns where the 1848 Public Health Act was adopted and a local board set up (see pp. 52, 138). Here again superb large scale plans were drawn up; indeed one of the criticisms of the General Board was that it commissioned unnecessarily detailed surveys (again on a ten foot scale) merely to identify problems of drainage and housing, which slowed down any remedial action and added to the cost of adopting the Act. For those towns included in these surveys, however, they are another superb source for urban topography, which can be compared with the plans of the 1870s and possibly used for 'house repopulation' in conjunction with the 1871 or 1881 census (pp. 34, 85).

This section has outlined those resources of the Ordnance Survey which the beginner is likely to make use of. For more advanced work the OS has various services which may be of interest, such as the supply of unpublished survey data, and has some archival material, relating for example to boundaries and land utilisation, which is worth investigating. The latest OS catalogue is the best guide to the former, while there is a growing technical literature on early OS plans.

Tithe maps

Whereas in towns Ordnance Survey plans may carry the history of large-scale mapping back to the 1840s, in rural areas the next stage back from the second edition of the OS will be the tithe map, one of the local historian's most basic tools (Fig. 4, p. 103)

Tithe, a render of one-tenth of the produce of land to the local church, was payable in England from early medieval times, as village churches were established by private landholders. Normally, the builder of such a church would assign to the parson the tithes of the land over which he was lord, i.e. the manor. The parson was responsible for cure of souls in the area from which he received tithe, i.e. his parish. Thus arose the correspondence in many parts of the country between manor and parish boundaries. The coincidence was not universal: in some parishes estates were divided and there might be two or more manors in the village; in other cases a manor might extend over all or part of several parishes. But in large parts of southern England parish boundaries, before they began to be changed by the building of new churches in the nineteenth century, or by statutory reform of local government, represent not only the boundaries of very old ecclesiastical units, dating from the building of the village church in the eleventh or twelfth century, but possibly even older estate boundaries, perhaps of the tenth century. In the North, township boundaries are of similar antiquity, while in Wales so much less is known of early territorial organisation or the building of medieval churches that it is more difficult to determine the age of parish or hamlet boundaries. In all parts of the country, however, the boundaries shown on tithe maps are important historical documents in their own right, and a good clue to early estate boundaries as well as those of the local church. Inexplicable deviations by a boundary from what would seem its 'natural' course along a stream or the side of a wood may have an early medieval explanation, while the survival of detached 'islands' of one parish within the land of another (swept away by statute later in the nineteenth century) may reflect a Domesday or even older division of a vill between two estates.

Although originally tithe income was assigned to the parson of the church, in many parishes the 'advowson' of the living (the right to appoint the priest, which normally belonged to the man who built the church) was granted in the twelfth or thirteenth century to a religious house, either local or further afield, and with the advowson went the tithes. An abbey, monastery or other house thus endowed would appoint a priest to serve the church thus appropriated, who was called a 'vicar' (from the Latin for 'deputy'), a secular clergyman who lived in the parish. They were remunerated by a share of the tithe income from the parish, usually about a third of the total (the 'small tithes') while everything else (the 'great tithes') went to the 'rector' (i.e. ruler) of the church, meaning not an individual but a religious corporation. Hence arose the distinction between two different kinds of beneficed incumbent, since in a parish where the living was not appropriated the parson himself was the rector. This distinction was maintained after the Dissolution, when tithes and advowsons owned by monasteries were sold by the crown along with their temporal property. In many cases, a local landowner acquired the tithes of his parish and possibly also the advowson, so that the parson still received only a small income while farmers in the village, who may well have been tenants of the tithe-owner, found themselves paying tithe to the same family rather than to the parson. The difference between vicars and rectors in the modern church is purely titular but until salaries replaced tithe as their main source of income the contrast in wealth and social standing could be considerable.

The early nineteenth-century campaign for tithe reform was concerned less with the position of the clergy than with the arbitrary and haphazard incidence of tithe. Traditionally payable in kind, tithe was normally rendered in cash by this period, but the amount was settled merely by a combination of local custom and willpower: an energetic impropriator or rector would extract more from reluctant tithe-payers than an absentee landowner or parson who relied on an agent for collection. More seriously, the purchaser of a farm or estate would not know certainly his liability to tithe on the land he acquired. To regularise the situation, and partly to meet the demands of opponents of tithe in any form, or those who viewed the accumulated wealth of the established church with hostility, the government in 1836 passed a Tithe Commutation Act. This provided for the conversion of tithe in every parish where a similar arrangement had not already been made (most often at the time of parliamentary enclosure perhaps fifty years earlier) from a payment in cash or kind to a 'rent-charge' on land, the amount varying according to the way in which the land was cultivated and the price of corn. A rent-charge is termed by lawyers an 'incorporeal hereditament', a piece of real property that exists but cannot be seen. Whoever received the tithes, rector, vicar, perpetual curate or impropriator, would henceforth receive a tithe rent-charge, divided in many parishes between vicar and impropriator in the same proportions as before.

Following the model of the Poor Law Amendment Act (p. 51) the Act of 1836 established a Tithe Commission in London: this dispatched assistant commissioners around the country to operate the Act, which affected about two-thirds of England and virtually all Wales. In each parish an assistant commissioner established the local facts by holding public meetings, commissioned a survey, and drew up a provisional agreement between the tithe owners as to the rent-charge payable to each, according to previous practice and the new legislation. This agreement was then confirmed by the commissioners. The process obviously took time to implement and most tithe awards under the 1836 Act date from the 1840s, with a few from before 1840 or after 1850.

The best known product of this process is the award drawn up by the assistant commissioner. After it had been confirmed, the award formed part of the archives of the Tithe Commission, which are now part of the Inland Revenue group at the Public Record Office (p. 139). Two official copies were made, and sometimes further private copies, which may occasionally be printed, whereas the official texts were in manuscript. One copy was kept in the parish to which the award related and a second was sent to the diocesan bishop. These copies are for most purposes as reliable as the one held by the Tithe Commission, although strictly speaking only those bearing the Commission's seal, as opposed to the signature of a commissioner, were accepted as first class copies.

The award consisted of two parts, a written agreement commuting the tithes of the parish, establishing the total rent-charge payable in lieu and dividing it between the tithe owners, and a schedule, setting out how much of the total rent-charge was payable on every parcel of land in the parish that was subject to tithe. Not all land was titheable: the built-up core of medieval towns was often tithe free, as was land owned in the middle ages by certain religious houses. Sometimes land not subject to tithe was scheduled separately, together with the reason for exemption, usually given as 'prescription', which amounted to admitting that tithe had never been paid on this land and its present owners had no intention of abandoning this privilege.

The need to schedule every parcel of land in the parish, at least outside a medieval borough, is what gives a tithe award its incomparable value to the topographer. Since there were no large-scale OS plans in 1836, surveys had to be commissioned specially for each tithe award, on a scale large enough to show every parcel, with each one numbered and keyed to the schedule. The scale chosen was usually between 12 and 25 inches to the mile. The maps had only to mark the boundaries of each parcel and are less detailed than OS plans, with few place-names and most buildings merely blocked-in rather than drawn in full. On the other hand, tithe maps recorded early medieval parish boundaries and islands of tithe-free former monastic land, as well as a host of modern features, which had been lost by the 1870s. Above all, they have a full written schedule accompanying them describing the land in far more detail than an OS fieldbook.

The schedules attached to tithe awards were not compiled in such detail for the benefit of historians nor to provide a local register of landowners and occupiers, although awards were used in this way. Each column in the schedule had some practical administrative purpose in the 1840s and together they provide the fullest picture of the local landscape one can normally obtain from anywhere, especially in a parish with poor estate records. First of all, the parcel numbers on the map were used to identify parcels in the schedules, with a written description alongside. The latter may be a field-name, making tithe awards an invaluable source for modern names which can be found also in deeds and possibly related to much earlier forms of the same name; or it may be a term such as 'Homestead' (i.e. farmhouse), 'Barn, Stables, Yard &c', 'Ironworks, Furnaces, Foundry, Kilns &c', 'Mill, Leat, Mill Holme &c'; or it may be the word 'Field' written dozens of times, with no names and just a gap where one might have hoped for a precise description of industrial premises. Not all awards are as full as others.

A discovery which frequently disappoints the new user of tithe awards is that the parcel numbers are not arranged numerically in the schedule. If you are seeking the owner and occupier of a particular field or building it is not normally possible to turn quickly from the map to the appropriate place in the award; you have to search through the book until you spot the parcel number in one of the middle columns. Particularly enthusiastic extramural classes have been known to rewrite thousand-parcel tithe awards in numerical order to make them easier to use, and if you are contemplating sustained work on a tithe map, it may be worth indexing the schedule in some way. A schedule is normally arranged in alphabetical order of owner, with each tenant listed in the same order under his landlord's name. Institutional owners such as the parish, turnpike trust or chapel trustees generally come at the end. As with land tax assessments (p. 59), the terms 'owner' and 'occupier' can be accepted at face value by the beginner, but are open to some qualification. 'Owners' can include long leaseholders; they can also include the trustees of an estate subject to a marriage settlement or trustees of an owner who was under age. Occupiers are not always given in full, especially for cottages, where 'John Smith and others' occupying '12 Cottages, Premises &c' should if possible be checked with the census enumerator's book to find the names of the other 23 householders. A problem with Welsh awards, arising from the different tradition of personal nomenclature in that country, is that of establishing whether the names in the first two columns are given as 'John Smith' or 'Smith, John' when some appear as 'Evan Evan' and others as 'Evan, Evan'. The general rule seems to be that owners' names are inverted, tenants' names are not, but if your are hoping to link a tithe award to other records it is important to note the names correctly.

Other columns in the award give the acreage and state of cultivation of each parcel (occasionally actual crops are named), necessary since the Act laid down a different level of rent-charge for arable, meadow and pasture, and the amount payable to the tithe-owner or owners, the latter probably the information least used by local historians. There is finally a 'Remarks' column, used sometimes to note subsequent changes in ownership, the disappearance of a field under a railway line or, at least in the Tithe Commission copy, the redemption of the rent-charge by the landowner for a lump sum payment. In 1930 provision was made for the ultimate redemption of all remaining tithe rent-charge, a process that has now been completed for the whole country.

If you are simply looking at a tithe map to trace the existence or non-existence of a particular feature, such as your own house, plus its owner or occupier in 1840, then a visit to inspect the most accessible copy of the award will usually be sufficient. Apart from the complete set of central government copies at Kew there should be a diocesan copy at the local record office (the National Library in Wales), and the parish copy may have been deposited there also, either by the church or the parish council. The latter is the copy most likely to have disappeared or to be in poor condition; if you are planning to have the map or schedule copied the diocesan copy is often the best to go for. In Wales, this is invariably the case, partly because the National Library has such good map-copying facilities. Only in desperation order a copy from the PRO, since it will be very expensive.

If you are interested in exploring the history of your parish in depth, especially its landscape history, it is undoubtedly worth getting a complete copy of the tithe award, map and schedule, since it probably offers more scope for further research, backwards from the 1840s into the pre-industrial landscape, forwards to later OS maps, and sideways to the census enumerators' books, than any other source. Many long winter evenings can happily be devoted to exploring all the facets of the tithe map for your village, which you are unlikely to have time to appreciate fully on a visit to the record office. The slowest and cheapest way to make a copy is to trace the plan and write out the schedule by hand, abbreviating terms for the state of cultivation of each field and probably omitting the columns listing rent-charge payable. If you do make a tracing of the tithe map, preferably on plastic film rather than paper, a local plan-copying shop will be able to make cheap dyeline copies for under 50p a time, on which you can colour in particular features, such as ownership and occupation or land usage. If you have the plan copied photographically ask the record office if it can be done on to drawing film rather than document paper, since it can then be dyelined. If you end up with an ordinary paper copy, either a photograph or a wad of A3 xeroxes which have to be stuck together (preferably with studio gum rather than sellotape) a plan-copying firm can still make a reproducible master on film but it will cost much more (say £20 for an A1 sheet) because they will have to make a negative. The essential point is that it is worth getting a copy of the tithe map, with parcel numbers, in a form from which cheap, if not entirely permanent, copies can be made so that you can explore several lines of enquiry separately.

A slightly different approach, which may be useful for those parishes in upland Britain where the tithe map resembles a Persian carpet and fills half the searchroom, is to transcribe detail from the map on to a photocopy of the first edition six-inch OS map of the 1870s. In most country areas there will not have been much change during the intervening period, and you will then have a more convenient digest of the older map which can be related directly to later editions of the OS. For small areas, transcribing detail on to a 25 inch plan may also be simpler than having part of the tithe map copied. In all cases like this, where you have a master map with crucial detail for the area you are working on, it is often worth making an initial investment at a local plan-printing bureau to have the map copied on to plastic film, since dyeline copies are so much simpler to make than sectional photocopies and much cheaper than large-format xeroxing. Dyeline copies do not last for ever, but they are so cheap that new copies can be made more or less as needed.

The schedules attached (or formerly attached) to tithe maps are not easy to copy on ordinary office machines, especially if they are still tightly rolled round or inside a plan. On a large xerox machine, they will reduce beautifully to A3 size and remain completely legible, but not all record offices have this equipment. Some may insist that their tithe awards can only be microfilmed, possibly by an outside firm at some expense. If you do acquire film in this way, it is now fairly easy to find a microfilm reader that will also make photocopies, preferably up to A3 size, on which to produce hard copy of your tithe award. For a long-term project, it is worth transcribing the schedule almost in full, either in the record office or at home from photocopies, using a separate sheet for each *occupier's* holding. These can then be sorted by occupier as opposed to owner and the occupiers traced in other contemporary records, especially the census. This operation also brings together all the land rented by one person from several different owners to give a tenant farmer's total acreage. The very keen individual or group may decide to make an index with a card for every parcel, so that they can be sorted by parcel number, or in alphabetical order of field-name, again adding cross-references to the cards from deeds or estate surveys (pp. 54–59) which mention the same name. This involves far more work, particularly for a large parish, and writing the names of the major owners a great many times.

Some of the uses to which you can put a tithe map and award have already been touched on. Essentially, they provide a virtually complete picture of your community from which to develop work in different directions. To begin with, it will probably be worth marking up different copies of the plan with field-names, the names of owners, the names of occupiers, and land usage. The latter can be compared with conditions today, a pleasant and not usually over-strenuous field exercise in a country parish, or in some parts of the country with a Land Utilization map of the 1940s. The value of using tithe map field-names to identify premises conveyed in stray deeds has already been mentioned (p. 59). Some mid-nineteenth-century deeds also use tithe map parcel numbers, usually superseded when the 25 inch OS became available. The same applies to rentals, terriers or other estate material surviving among landowners' muniments. Here the tithe map is especially useful, when there are no estate maps, in giving a topographical dimension to estate acquisitions and disposals recorded only in deeds. Using the summarised details of ownership and occupation at the end of the schedule, one can work out the division of landownership in the parish in the 1840s (Family A had 80 per cent of the land, Family B 10 per cent, and so on) or the average size of farms, including variation between mixed farms and those with no arable, or between those on the main estate and owner occupied freeholds.

The tithe map is useful for much more besides the history of farming and landownership. Industrial premises may be mapped on a large scale here and nowhere else, and details of ownership and occupation given, useful in tracing documentary material where no business records survive (p. 67). If you are interested in the history of your house, or of every house in the village, the tithe map is almost always the best place to start, largely because of the ownership and tenancy information it supplies. If your house (which typically will have no deeds before 1930) proves to have been part of a local estate in 1840 that may again be a key to locating deeds or other documents (p. 54). Since most farmhouse and cottage building was entirely traditional up to 1840, the tithe map is a good place to begin a survey of local vernacular architecture (p. 123). Note each building on the tithe map on a more recent map and see how many survive, either at all or relatively unaltered. See how many of the farms of 1840 are still working agricultural holdings, perhaps looking also at old six-inch maps to see when farmhouses were abandoned as such.

Most of these suggestions relate to a rural community, but tithe maps are also invaluable for the surburban topographer. Many towns show little suburban sprawl by 1840; certainly what are now the outer London surburbs were simply villages at this date. Here the pattern of landownership as revealed by the tithe map is often the key to what happened in the 1890s or 1930s. Try transcribing the boundaries of tithe map estates on to a 25 inch plan post-dating the main period of suburban growth. You may find that the network of avenues, closes and drives fits into the pattern of landownership two generations earlier, or that parts of the parish, inexplicably developed much earlier or much later than their neighbours, belonged to one particular owner in 1840. From here you may be able to trace a sale catalogue of 1920 advertising the estate as desirable building land, or the first deed belonging to your 1936 semi may be a conveyance from a descendant of the owner in the tithe award to Wimpey or New Ideal Homes. For earlier suburbs, it may become clear that by the 1880s the mansion had been let, the family were living in South Kensington and so land was shaved off the edge of the old deer park to make way for Beech Villas or Laburnum Lodge, for which the oldest deed is a 99 year building lease reserving a ground rent to the landowner.

For older built-up areas tithe awards can be disappointing. The core of medieval boroughs was often tithe-free and the map will simply outline the area and give it a single parcel number described in the schedule as 'Town of Barchester'. For some towns, however, there are very detailed tithe awards, in which the schedule lists the contents of each plot ('House, Overgateway, Workshops, Dye-House, Boiler House, Steam Engine, Wash-House, Bakery, Croft and Premises' is quite possible), which, with the information about ownership and occupation, are an invaluable starting-point for any exploration of earlier or later history. Infilling of medieval burgage plots behind the main street frontage, thus creating slum 'courts' and 'yards', can be traced by comparing the tithe map (on which there may be very little infill) with a large-scale plan of the 1870s (on which there may be a great deal, perhaps christened 'Pleasant View', or 'Robinson's Row' after the owner shown on the tithe map). The function of many nineteenth-century factory buildings can be identified from an urban tithe award, which may also be the key to locating on the ground property conveyed in miscellaneous deeds in solicitors' collections, if one of them supplies the name of an owner or occupier in the 1840s.

The other major use to which both urban and rural tithe awards can be put is for what has come to be called 'house repopulation': trying to identify on the tithe map all the householders who appear in one of the census enumerators' books now available (1841–81). Most commonly, one uses either 1841 or 1851, probably the latter, even if the tithe award is nearer in date to 1841, because the second census conducted by the Registrar General was much more carefully compiled and the replies are somewhat more detailed. Census enumerators' books have been described (p. 34), as have tithe awards, and in theory it is simple to find the same occupier in both and locate his house on the map and then on the ground, especially as census enumeration normally had an underlying topographical basis. In practice, it is often rather difficult, and few who have tried this with a place of any size have managed to locate every household in the census on the tithe map. Sometimes an enumerator did not copy schedules into his book systematically, or did not give sufficiently detailed addresses in built-up areas. There may have been too much change between 1840 and 1851, so that whole streets in the census do not appear on the map. Most commonly, however, there are just too many households in the census compared with the tithe map, even after allowing for new building. This is where the deficiencies of the tithe award's list of occupiers become obvious. Head leaseholders may appear in the award, whereas the census will list a dozen undertenants renting all or part of the house; 'Several' is not unknown as a name in the 'Occupier' column of a schedule. The easiest community in which to tackle house repopulation is an upland parish in which settlement was dispersed, all the farms were individually named in both the tithe award and the census, and, if most of them were freeholders, there is little change over a ten-year period. In tightly packed nucleated villages where 'Glebe Cottage', 'The Old Chantry', 'Maltings' and such names date from c. 1970 and there are no house names in the census it is much more difficult, as it is in small towns, which is where there is most likely to be a surfeit of census over tithe households.

These comments should not discourage the local investigator from trying house repopulation in his own community, since it makes a satisfying change from the *Daily Telegraph* crossword and residents of Glebe Cottage now are invariably entertained to know who lived there in 1851. It may even induce them to let you see their deeds, which will allow you to work out a full history of the house. What is needed, apart from complete copies of both the census and tithe award and a good deal of time and patience, is local knowledge, full use of other material, especially directories and electoral registers (pp. 30, 65), and a few stable landmarks to start with, such as pubs on street corners, which will be clearly identifiable in several records. A complete project of this kind makes it possible to give a geographical dimension to all the questions one can ask of census material (pp. 36–9) and fleshes out what is known of the occupiers of farms in the 1840s from the tithe map alone. House-repopulation and other work on the tithe map and census can also make an attractive and fairly simple publication for an individual or local group wishing to interest people in the recent past, since so many surviving houses will be described in such a booklet or trail.

The tithe map may be the earliest complete survey of your parish, and possibly the only one before the 1870s. The local historian working on a community where tithe was commuted before 1836 may find, however, that the absence of a tithe award is balanced by a detailed and somewhat earlier enclosure award. These, and other pre-1840 material, are considered in the next section.

Enclosure awards, estate surveys and other maps

Maps drawn up in connection with parliamentary *enclosure* in the eighteenth and nineteenth centuries are often coupled in textbooks with tithe maps. This is misleading, since they are much less numerous than awards under the 1836 Act and despite superficial similarity of arrangement, with a plan marking numbered parcels keyed to an accompanying schedule, they are rather different in scope and generally less comprehensive.

After about 1750 a local Act of Parliament became a common device for carrying out, usually on a larger scale than previously, a process that had gone on in all communities since time immemorial, the 'enclosure' of land. Enclosure does not begin with the parliamentary enclosure movement of this period; on the contrary, this marks its final phase, ending in growing opposition to further destruction of common land. Whether by local Act, general Act, agreement enrolled in one of the central courts or simply private agreement, enclosure describes one of two operations affecting land usage in a community. It might mean enlarging the area of land within a parish that was 'cultivated' in the widest sense (it may only have become permanent pasture after enclosure, not arable or meadow) by dividing the common land between the freeholders of the manor: or it might mean the rearrangement of existing arable land (and sometimes also meadow) so that each farmer henceforth cultivated his own land himself, rather than took part in a communal system based on large open fields in which each farmer had strips of land. The topographical effect of each form of enclosure was rather different, but the legal operation was basically similar. On a medieval manor all the tenants, free and unfree, had customary rights over what was legally known as 'waste'. This might be barren moorland which supported some summer grazing; or a 'village green' in the heart of the settlement used for recreation and the gathering of fuel as well as grazing animals; or alternatively an area of common near the village, of perhaps 50 or 100 acres. Between about 1750 and 1850, and especially during the period 1780–1820, millions of acres of such 'waste', the greater part of it moorland and mountain rather than village green, were enclosed under local Acts and the land divided between the owners of the existing enclosed land of the parish, the successors of the medieval free tenants of the manor. Acts of this kind were passed for parishes in every county in England and Wales, but particularly affected upland counties where more un-enclosed moorland had survived earlier land clearance.

In those parts of England where in the middle ages arable land was cultivated, in whole or in part, in a two- or three-field system of communal farming, with fields divided into unfenced strips, and where these fields had not already been swept away, a similar phase of parliamentary enclosure during the same period largely completed the process of enclosing common field arable. Instead of extending the area of cultivated land, the Act provided for the division of open fields into closes, and the allocation of closes to the freeholders in proportion to their previous holdings in the fields. This rearrangement of property rights was best enshrined, according to eighteenth-century opinion, in an Act of Parliament, and much of the remaining open field of Midland and Eastern England disappeared in this way. In the North and West and in Wales the much smaller proportion of arable cultivated in common in the middle ages had mostly been enclosed much earlier by private agreement, so that very few enclosure Acts for these regions are concerned with common field.

Both types of enclosure affected the pattern of landownership as well as land use, although how far parliamentary enclosure led to the disappearance of the small landowner is now less clear than was once supposed. But there was a tendency for large estates to grow larger and some small freeholders to disappear as such, as the local historian may discover in his own parish by comparing estate surveys of different dates or looking at land tax assessments, or comparing the number of owners in the tithe award with the number in an enclosure award fifty years before. The enclosure of both open field and common waste generally led to the building of new farms in a parish, which may well have left a fairly obvious architectural legacy today in the form of a group of buildings all clearly dating from the early nineteenth century. In open-field regions, these new farm-steads would be out in the former fields, and the older farms along the village street gradually declined into labourers' cottages. Where moorland was enclosed, new farms would be established on the former waste beyond the limits of medieval clearance, cultivating, or at least grazing, newly enclosed marginal land.

In the case of parishes where there was no enclosure by Act, or any other documentary evidence of enclosure, it is sometimes possible to trace the topographical results of early private enclosure by looking carefully at the tithe map for farms built 'out in the fields' away from a nucleated settlement. They often have names including the element 'Fields', most obviously 'Old Field Farm', meaning a medieval open field, not a close. For parishes where there is a parliamentary enclosure award, it may be possible to trace the same process from maps and documents.

After 1792 an enclosure award executed by commissioners named in a local Act had to be enrolled among the records of quarter sessions, so that it should now be in the county record office, although copies also turn up in parish chests and among estate muniments. In some counties the clerk of the peace also collected earlier awards. How extensive and thus how useful it will be for local landscape history depends on how thorough-going was the en-closure. Where a medieval three-field system had survived almost intact, as hundreds did in the Midland Plain, Lincolnshire and East Anglia, an award may include a map of the entire parish, illustrating the existing layout, with that proposed by the commissioners after enclosure superimposed on an open-field plan. Where only rem-nants of an open-field system survived from previous enclosure, they may show merely the area to be enclosed. The same is true of awards affecting only a village green, a small common, or strips of waste alongside the highway, which will be mapped as a series of sketches with adjoining land shown to identify the parcels affected. If several thousand acres were being enclosed on the edge of the parish, there may be an outline map of a more or less featureless moor, divided up into neat square blocks for the new owners to take up.

Where an enclosure award and a tithe map are both available, it is worth comparing the two, especially where the former was very sweeping. By transcribing detail from the enclosure map on to a copy of the tithe map you may be able to make a substantial leap backwards towards a picture of medieval land usage, removing half a dozen post-1780 farmsteads or a thousand acres of suspiciously square fields on the edge of the moor which form no part of the medieval topography of the parish. It is also worth pursuing the details of the enclosure award on the ground. As well as following up new farmsteads, one can look at new housing or industry which may have appeared on the enclosed waste that was of little agricultural value, or actually check that the process of enclosure took place as the commissioners intended. Some awards were not implemented for several years, and occasionally the economic margin to which it was worth enclosing land receded faster than the new owner could build fences, so that some waste was in fact never enclosed as an award said it should have been.

As well as dividing and allotting land, enclosure commissioners sometimes took the opportunity to straighten or lay out highways across land being enclosed, although they could not alter the arrangements on land already enclosed. The term 'highways' includes footpaths and bridlepaths, and since enclosure awards are public records which have always been in offical custody the evidence they supply as to the existence and status of rights of way is admissible in law. It is for this reason that archivists are sometimes pursued by property owners or ramblers seeking to deny or establish the existence of a right of way, or by local pony club enthusiasts hoping to have footpaths restored to bridlepath status. Awards are a useful source for the history of roads and tracks in a community (see also p. 70), since enclosure often led to substantial changes in their layout.

Quarter sessions records contain another class of enrolled *plans*, those which had to be *deposited* from 1792 with the clerk of the peace (and with parliament) in advance of an application to parliament to build a canal, turnpike road, railway, docks or certain other public works authorised by local Act. A copy of the plan had to be supplied to the clerk of every county through which the canal or railway would pass and plans were of course deposited for hundreds of schemes which were never proceeded with. Early canal and turnpike plans of the late eighteenth century are often on too small a scale to be of much value, but the older railway plans (up to about 1880, when most railway promotion was complete and companies simply adapted 25 inch plans instead of making new surveys) are much more detailed. All are useful for transport history (p. 67) but local historians not interested in canals or railways sometimes fail to appreciate their general value. The idea of having a plan publicly available was to allow landowners affected by a new scheme to see exactly where the line of the canal or railway fell and whose land would be affected. The plans are thus strip-maps, marking a line and at least a hundred yards on either side, with the parcels numbered and scheduled, and supplying the usual details (acreage, owner, occupier, usage) for a tract of county where a railway was built or proposed. In towns, where much property might have to be demolished for a new station, the plan would be drawn on a larger scale and would cover a wide area. For towns not otherwise well served by early plans it is worth checking those deposited for proposed railways to see if any has an inset providing an enlarged plan of part or all of the town, which will probably be superior to the tithe map and a generation earlier than the first edition 25 inch plan. Unfortunately, it is difficult to list deposited plans comprehensively so as to include every parish covered. Early schemes and those for the major lines that were actually executed usually stand out but in some offices a great many inevitably appear as 'Midland Railway, 1876. Additional Lines etc', which leaves a lot to the imagination.

Enclosure awards and deposited plans may be indexed separately in a record office, or they may be included in a general index of maps and plans, the rest of which are mainly in deposited collections. The most important maps in the latter category are *estate surveys*, touched on in the section on landownership (p. 55) and invaluable, used with other estate material, such as rental and deeds, for recreating the past landscape and the history of farming.

Medieval landholders did not commission maps of their property —to them a 'survey' meant a written account—but from the end of the sixteenth century to the middle of the nineteenth landowners employed surveyors to produce maps of their property, usually accompanied by a 'terrier' listing tenants and holdings. Since about 1870 large landowners, public and private, have normally relied on marking up 25 inch OS plans to identify their property. As with estate records generally, it is unwise to be over-optimistic in searching for surviving maps. Surveys were expensive and are more likely to have been made for large estates than small ones. They were not frequently re-done; surveys that have been heavily used in estate offices, and more especially their terriers, will often contain half a century of annotation and updating. Above all, they were not plans commissioned by munificent landowners who wished to provide the community with a beautifully coloured large-scale plan of their village; they are plans of what one person owned. Where this was most of the land in a parish, the map will amount to a parish map; in other cases it may simply consist of small sketches locating isolated parcels in parishes in which most of the land belonged to others. Since landownership tended to be heavily divided in old towns, estate maps are usually least informative for such places, whereas for some parishes from as early as 1600 there are some magnificent examples in local record offices, and important holdings at the Public Record office. The latter are catalogued in a published volume and are obviously strongest for towns with a service connection or estates owned by the Duchy of Lancaster or another adjunct of the crown.

However comprehensive or sketchy their coverage of a particular place, estate maps provide similar information for all the parishes included in a survey. The parcels shown on the plans are numbered or lettered and a schedule in one corner of the map, on facing pages of a volume, or in a separate book supplies the name of the tenant; the name, acreage and cultivation of each parcel; possibly the terms on which the land was held (at will, seven year lease etc); and sometimes comments about the holding. Where a landowner was planning changes, or acquired an estate that appeared to have been neglected, the surveyor was often asked to report, either separately or in the terrier, on possible improvements in buildings, tenants, tenures and land usage, which can sometimes be very illuminating.

It is possible, on a large estate, to find two or more surveys at different dates; more typically there will be one eighteenth-century map, either a single sheet or part of an atlas. Many, with extensive use of colour and elaborate cartouches and scales, are objects of great beauty. It may be worth tracing the map, if it provides a comprehensive picture of your village, or transcribing the detail on to a copy of the tithe map or the six-inch Ordnance Survey. An eighteenth-century map may be a better source of field-names than the tithe map; it may portray a landscape that had been much altered by industry by 1840 before such changes began; or it may show a landscape about to be privately enclosed or emparked. Comparison of an estate map with a tithe survey may reveal the disappearance of individual houses or a whole village, or the earlier map may show a moated site that had become 'Mote Croft' by 1840, with indeterminate earthworks surviving on the ground. Some estate maps, especially those of the seventeenth century, purport to show houses as bird's-eye sketches, apparently in realistic detail. In a village where much farmhouse and cottage architecture has survived from the period of the Great Rebuilding (c. 1540–1700), it may be possible to compare such drawings with standing structures to judge whether they can be relied upon for those buildings that have disappeared. Attempts to link the evidence of sketches to the numbers of hearths in tax assessments (p. 134) are rather less convincing.

Most local historians have some interest in the history of the landscape and for such an investigation maps are obviously essential. The best way of proceeding is probably to start with a sequence of Ordnance Survey six-inch maps to see how the picture has changed over the last century, then look at all the evidence for landowner-ship, farming and land usage which the tithe map can provide. If there is any earlier map material for the parish this can often best be transcribed on to a tithe map base, so that it can be related directly to firm nineteenth-century evidence. Working in this way you will be able to produce a series of maps from the present back to at least 1840, and then with luck 'peel away' relatively modern features from the tithe map towards a speculative but reasoned view of the landscape in medieval times. An enclosure map redrawn to tithe map scale will enable you to remove post-enclosure closes and farmsteads; a deposited plan will show what the area was like before a canal was built; either source may locate pre-turnpike or pre-enclosure roads.

To carry the history of the landscape further back will involve the use of other, more specialised evidence: the clues supplied by field-names and minor place-names for the former existence of open fields where these were not mapped before enclosure; archaeological evidence for deserted, shrunken or moved settlements; former tracks not marked on any map; medieval industrial sites indicated only by slight earthworks. Material of this kind is discussed in the next chapter and by combining fieldwork with the careful study of maps it should be possible for any community, urban or rural, to produce at least an outline sketch-plan of the parish in medieval times. In a publication, either standing alone in a booklet on landscape history or as part of a chapter on the middle ages in a larger parish study, a map of this kind, with a commentary on how it was compiled, is likely to be of much greater interest than a reiteration of unconnected references to the same place from printed medieval public records, which is what so much old-fashioned writing on local communities in the middle ages consisted of.

Although the main map sources have now been described, it may be worth concluding with brief references to some other material found in either libraries or record offices. The oldest local maps are those published by Christopher Saxton, John Speed and their imitators in the sixteenth and seventeenth centuries. These are of decorative rather than practical interest, since the scale is too small to mark any local features, but they may be of value as evidence of the existence or not of a park, if their inclusion or omission of this feature can be relied upon. John Speed's *county maps* of 1610 mostly have sketch plans of the county town in one corner, which if redrawn with caution on to modern base material can provide a starting-point for urban topography. They provide in almost every case the earliest plan of the town in question, giving what is probably a fairly reliable guide to the layout of the medieval borough. County maps of this period are readily available as cheap reprints; another early map source reprinted in recent years is John Ogilvy's *road atlas* of 1675, the ancestor of all route maps in strip form. The atlas only covers main roads, but if the place you are interested in lay on a pre-industrial highway the maps are worth consulting. For anyone interested in a wider pattern of communications the atlas provides a sometimes surprising picture of what were then considered the major regional highways, not all of which survived as such into the turnpike era.

The maps of Saxton and his successors were only superseded in the second half of the eighteenth century, when a group of mapmakers resurveyed the country to produce new county maps on a scale of one inch to the mile or larger (Figs 1 and 2, pp. 98–101).

Virtually all English counties and most in Wales have a map of this period, which culminated in Christopher and John Greenwood's series of one-inch maps of the 1820s. There are the immediate predecessors of the one-inch Old Series of the Ordnance Survey (p. 73) and the best are of comparable quality. Only the larger scale maps claim to show every field (and then with questionable accuracy) but even on a one-inch scale it was possible, in the relatively uncrowded landscape of the late eighteenth century, to mark water-mills and other industrial features, turnpike roads, canals, country houses and parks. Copies of a county map of this period are usually available in both libraries and record offices and may have been reprinted commercially or by a local society, preferably with an analytical introduction. For towns, especially the larger eighteenth-century cities and ports, there may be privately published large-scale plans, which again have often been included in reprint projects. Smaller plans were sometimes published in town histories of the early nineteenth century and form part of a sequence of urban topography that begins with Speed and continues to the 1:500 OS plans of the 1870s (p. 77). Finally, for rural parishes the record office may have a plan with numbered parcels dating from some time in the decade after 1815, when an Act provided for a reform of the system of local rates which entailed new surveys being made. The origin of these rating plans is not always clear from the maps themselves.

Local historians interested in maps are generally well served by finding-aids, because the material is in such demand in libraries and record offices. There is usually at least a card index to the holdings of a particular repository and for several counties a published handlist or a full-scale bibliography. At an early stage in almost any research project, therefore, the local historian should check what map sources there are for his area. As with manuscripts, it is probably best to work backwards from current Ordnance Survey maps through the older editions of the larger OS scales and then try to relate the evidence of earlier privately produced maps to the first six-inch or 25 inch sheet for the same area. Taken in isolation, a scrappy eighteenth-century estate plan or a small-scale deposited plan for an early canal may seem impossible to relate to the present-day topography of the same area. When examined as the last, rather than first, stage in a step-by-step exploration of the landscape, however, it will fit in more easily and may supply clues as to the appearance of the same stretch of country centuries earlier. Not only are maps, especially such major sources as the tithe maps of the 1840s, invaluable for the general history of a community, but they add an extra dimension to almost any kind of more specialised enquiry. It is surprising, for example, how few genealogists seem to make any use of old maps to give a sense of place to their research and to see what a village looked like when their ancestors were enumerated there in

1871. Even fewer think of looking at tithe awards, which name dozens, sometimes hundreds of heads of household. Similarly with local historians interested in a particular house or some industrial building: even if all else fails, the place will always be on the Ordnance Survey map and probably on the tithe map, in which case you will have the names of owner and occupier on which to hang further enquiries. Maps are all-important in local history and they are also great fun.

Illustrations

Figure 1 Extract from P. P. Burdett's map of Derbyshire (2nd edition, 1791) showing the key to conventional signs used on the map and a stretch of country close to the Nottinghamshire border in mid-Derbyshire. Originally published at a scale of one inch to a mile, Burdett's county map is fairly typical of publications of this period, showing major landscape features (woods, commons etc) and certain types of building (seats, mills, churches etc). There is no attempt at this scale to mark individual fields and the representation of built-up areas is conventional.

Figure 2 Burdett's plan of Derby, forming an inset to his county map of 1767 (revised 1791). Although a town of 10,000 people in the 1801 census, Derby was still largely confined to its medieval core in this period, with fields, orchards and gardens running right up to the edge of the town. Most eighteenth-century county maps included a plan of the main town, which is often the first new survey since John Speed's of 1610.

Figure 3. The surveyor's drawing (at two inches to the mile) for part of the Ordnance Survey 'Old Series' one-inch map of Glamorgan. The drawing probably dates from about 1810 and includes field boundaries, which were not published on the final engraved map. Some minor place-names also disappeared between survey and publication.

Figure 4 Extract from the tithe map of 1840 for Llanblethian (S. Glamorgan), the village which appears towards the centre of OS drawing (Fig. 3) but is here shown in much more detail. The Llanblethian tithe map is typical of many for nucleated villages in that it supplies the first large-scale plan identifying individual houses, of which more details can be found by looking up the parcel numbers in the schedule (see p. 80). On the other hand, tithe maps rarely contain many place-names and provide a rather 'flat' featureless picture of settlement and landscape.

Figure 5 Ordnance Survey six-inch map, first edition (1879), of Llanblethian and Cowbridge (see also Figs. 3 and 4). The main contrast with the tithe map is the much greater wealth of place-names and landscape detail on the OS map, with woodland and common clearly distinguished. The actual field boundaries have hardly changed since 1840, nor has the built-up area.

Figure 6 An early panoramic photograph of Llanblethian, probably from about the same period as the first edition six-inch map. This view, which looks north across the valley in which the village lies, brings to life the landscape shown in the map, emphasising how much scattered timber there was around the village and highlighting the contrast between the three large houses to the right and below the church (The Cross, Hill House and Llanblethian Cottage) and the smaller cottages in the main part of the village. The large building towards the bottom left was a malthouse, which has now disappeared without trace, so that this photograph is the only evidence for its exact size and shape.

Figure 7 A six-inch map of an urban area (Chesterfield, Derbys) from the 1901 revision of the Ordnance Survey. This is a useful scale for giving a general view of a small but expanding town, whose medieval core around the church and market place (where the building is shaded somewhat more densely) was now surrounded by new suburbs to the north and west and railways and industry to the south and east, plus a municipal park with cricket ground and boating lake.

Figure 8 An extract from the 25-inch Ordnance Survey plan of 1876 showing the market place in Chesterfield (cf. Fig. 7), with its large open area (the result of twelfth-century replanning) now dominated by a market hall of 1857. To the east of the market place is a block of medieval 'shambles' (butchers' quarter) whose plan survives largely unaltered, and to the north and south of the market are medieval burgage plots with narrow street frontages and long rear crofts. By the 1870s these had been heavily infilled with slum housing and small workshops but would originally have accommodated gardens, stables, pig-sties and the like. The name 'Dog Kennels' apparently derived from early nineteenth-century subscription kennels in one of the yards.

Figure 9 This section of the Ordnance Survey 1:500 scale town plan of the 1870s shows a small part of Chesterfield market place (cf. Fig. 8) with the heads of burgage plots along Low Pavement and the Victorian market hall. The extract illustrates the enormous amount of detail published at this scale, including not only interior plans of public buildings but also a variety of street furniture. The gas plugs were for market stalls erected to the right of the hall two days a week.

Figure 10 A striking modern aerial photograph of a superficially uninteresting suburban landscape on the western outskirts of Chesterfield. In fact, the picture contains features illustrating every aspect of the history of the area from the middle ages onwards. At the top right hand corner allotment gardens overlie medieval open fields, bounded by a brook (indicated by denser vegetation above the gasholder) which was also a manorial boundary. The main road at the foot of the picture is a turnpike built about 1810 on a new line, along which a suburb grew up. The older houses on the road have backyards with workshops and sheds, which give way to smaller, neater terraces of late Victorian artisan cottages with tiny gardens. The gasholder and the textile mills below it (1860 and later) are signs of local industry; on the opposite edge of the picture is a Victorian board school with characteristic gothic windows and steep roofs. The inter-war council houses, built in rows of three with fairly generous gardens, plus other more recent building near the top of the photograph, complete the development of the area.

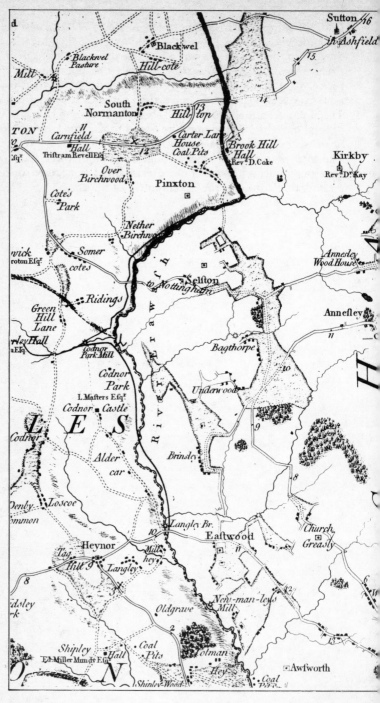

Figure 1

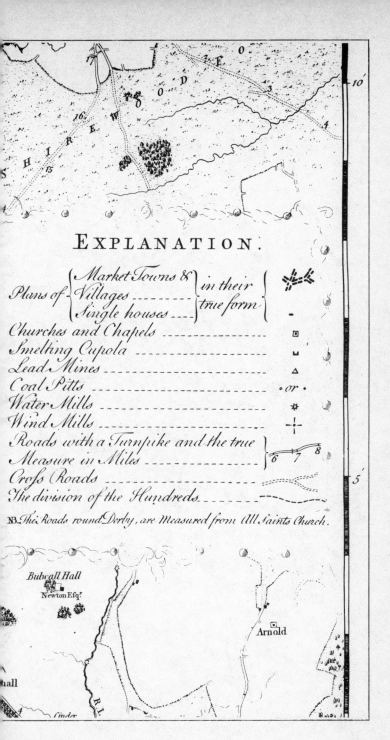

EXPLANATION.

Plans of { Market Towns & Villages ----- Single houses ---- } in their true form	
Churches and Chapels ----------------	
Smelting Cupola ----------------------	
Lead Mines --------------------------	
Coal Pitts ---------------------------	• or •
Water Mills --------------------------	
Wind Mills ---------------------------	
Roads with a Turnpike and the true Measure in Miles ---------------- } 6 7 8	
Cross Roads --------------------------	
The division of the Hundreds ----------	

N.B. The Roads round Derby, are Measured from All Saints Church.

Bulwell Hall
Newton Esq.ʳ

Arnold

hall

R.L.

Cinder

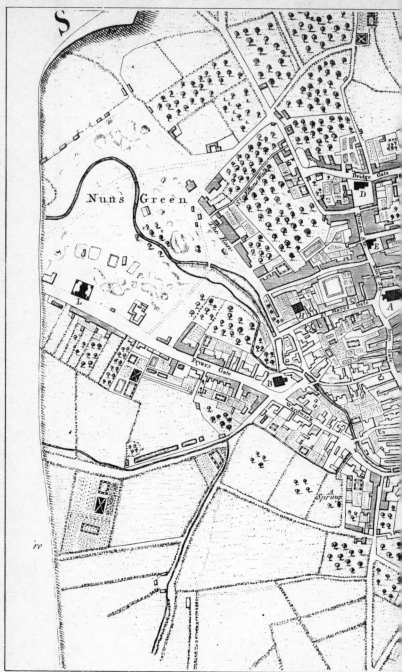

Figure 2

A. *All Saints* ……….
B. *St Werberghs* ……
C. *St Peters* ……….
D. *St Alkmunds* ……
E. *St Michaels* …….
F. *Silk Mills* ……….
G. *China Works* …….
H. *County Hall* ……
I. *Town Hall* ……..
K. *Assembly Room* ..
L. *Jail* …………….

To Nottingham

R I V E R

Ferry House

Copper Mills

H o l m s

Iron Mills

Cock pit Hill

Wharf

Pot Work

Castle Fields

Lock

50'

45'

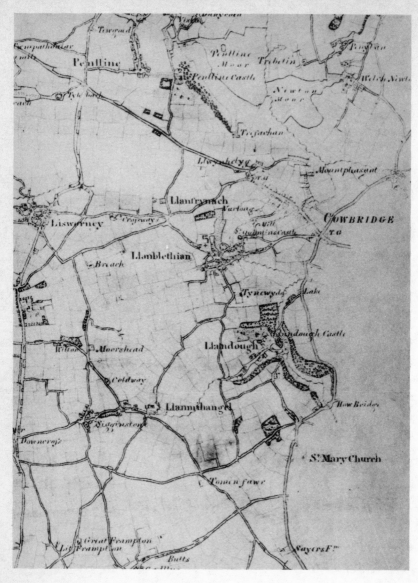

Figure 3

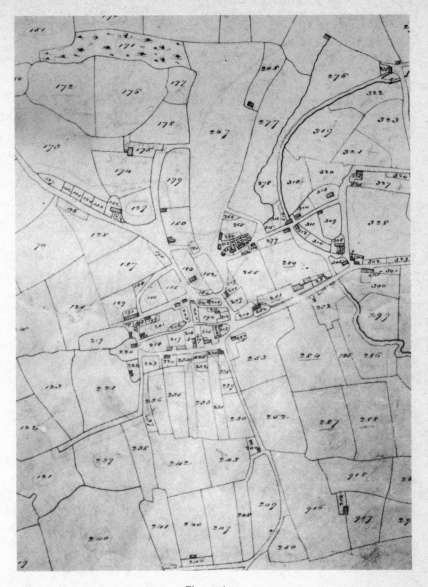

Figure 4

103

Figure 5 *left*

Figure 6 *above*

Figure 7

Figure 8

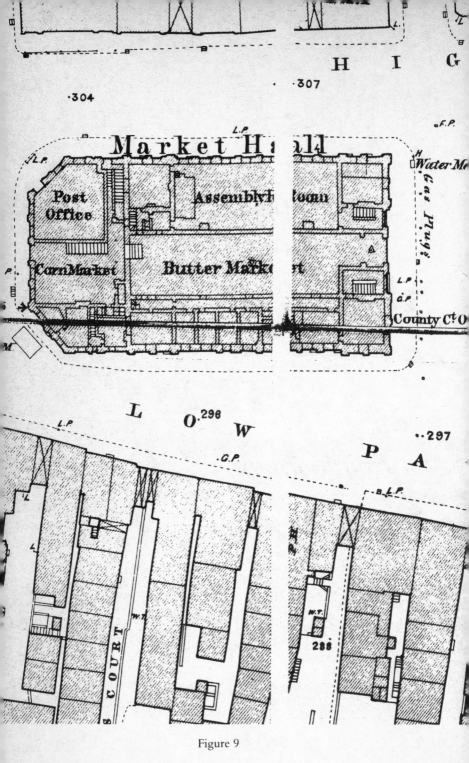

Figure 9

Figure 10

Chapter Five
LANDSCAPES AND BUILDINGS

Trends and structures

The last chapter set out the main map sources available to local historians and suggested some ways in which evidence of this kind could be used, to trace either individual features or the development of the landscape as a whole. It is now conventional wisdom to emphasise that maps and documents are only half the story and that for a complete picture one must also look at the landscape itself and buildings therein. This fascination with visual evidence on the part of English antiquaries is not new; what has changed, gradually since the beginning of the present century and much more rapidly in the last thirty years, is the way in which the study of physical evidence has erected itself into a separate discipline, which has in turn split into a number of different fields of varying academic value. To try to bring them all back together it became popular a few years ago to argue for 'total archaeology' or, if you were an historian, 'total history', terms which would have seemed strange to an eighteenth- or nineteenth-century antiquary, for whom there was no dichotomy between 'monuments and muniments' and who was equally at home with either. At local level, in field clubs or among the curators of museums, there is still no real division, but on a grander level several new fields of study have emerged, allegedly with their own techniques and invariably with their own journals.

The first change was the extension of archaeological research beyond the limits achieved by Haverfield and his contemporaries before the first world war, through which the archaeology of Roman Britain became an acceptable companion for prehistoric archaeology. In the next generation the value of archaeological evidence for the period 500–1100 became established; after the last war the same discipline extended its scope to the sixteenth century. A smaller group subsequently promoted 'post-medieval archaeology', urging the use of physical evidence as an adjunct to sixteenth-, seventeenth- or eighteenth-century history.

Meanwhile a changing view of society led to new interests in the field of architectural history, which in the nineteenth century established itself as a scholarly study less by the attention paid to documents than by the development of the measured drawing as a means of recording standing structures. From the turn of the century, but much more so after 1945, architectural historians became interested not only in churches, manor houses and public buildings, but in the homes of the mass of the people, the farmhouses and cottages which survived in most parts of Britain from the sixteenth century or later. Thus was 'vernacular architecture' born, concerned with buildings made of local materials by local craftsmen uninfluenced by conventions of 'polite' design. Its main field of study has remained the period from the sixteenth century, when the bulk of the population appear for the first time to have lived in houses intended to last more than a single generation, to the nineteenth, when the coming of the railways meant that building materials could be distributed nationally and the design of working-class housing ceased to vary greatly between different regions. Before the sixteenth century peasant houses have normally to be investigated archaeologically. In fact, the close links between those interested in standing structures and those who have come to this period from an interest in excavation have led to a hybrid approach which owes as much to archaeology as to architectural recording. A similar technique has been applied to medieval churches, where these are available for thorough study: the standing structure is stripped archaeologically and excavations may be conducted both inside and outside the walls of the building.

Many of those involved in medieval and post-medieval archaeology and the study of vernacular architecture have also been concerned with the promotion of 'landscape history'. Here the emphasis is on the 'total landscape', on trying to reconstruct what a particular stretch of country looked like a hundred, five hundred, a thousand or three thousand years ago. Again, this is not really a new pursuit, but in recent years it has attracted sufficient support to establish another national society and another journal. As its practitioners argue, landscape history involves the application of several disciplines to the same, usually fairly limited, area. The material of landscape history includes the results of archaeological excavation or the recording of earthworks or other field monuments; the surveying of polite or vernacular buildings or other structures; the analysis of field- and place-names; the use of maps and topographical documents; and, if really tackled in depth, the use of material from several scientific disciplines, especially geology and botany. Like most of the activities described in this chapter, landscape history 'done properly' requires a range of skills not usually combined in one person and, if conducted over an area of any size, considerable resources. On the other hand—unlike, for example, archaeological excavation—it is also something the individual amateur can do on a more modest scale with useful results.

There is one other member of this family, the black sheep of the flock—'industrial archaeology'. This leapt to prominence in the early 1960s as a popular pastime in many parts of the country, with local groups and a national journal. From the start, industrial archaeology was a puzzle and much time and energy was wasted in pointless debates about its definition and scope. It was argued that industrial archaeology was like, for example, marine archaeology, concerned with industry in any period; in practice, most of its supporters were interested in the physical remains of the Industrial Revolution, which at the time were rapidly disappearing. Unfortunately, most of those who claimed to be interested in the field did little or nothing to record these physical remains, many of which have now gone for ever. Instead, when they were not arguing about whether or not Roman pottery kilns were part of their subject, they tended to spend their time photographing cast-iron mileposts, taking 'brass-rubbings' of manhole covers, or restoring derelict canals. Little of this contributed anything to our knowledge of eighteenth- or nineteenth-century economic history or even the history of technology. It did result in the preservation of some important buildings and structures which might otherwise have been lost, so that now many of the principal surviving monuments of the Industrial Revolution are as much visited as Hadrian's Wall, but industrial archaeology was not to the Industrial Revolution what medieval archaeology has been to medieval history. Those responsible for establishing the Society for Medieval Archaeology or its post-medieval companion generally came from one of two backgrounds. Either they were experienced in excavating earlier archaeological sites and applied these skills to later remains, or they were trained in recording standing remains, whether they were earthworks or buildings. In either case, one produces measured drawings, or at least field sketches, and photographs, irrespective of whether the remains have first to be excavated. This procedure, developed since archaeology became a separate discipline in the nineteenth century, somehow never appealed to the promoters of industrial archaeology. Much was said and written about methodology without its being realised that there were no 'techniques of industrial archaeology'. All that was wanted were drawings and photographs. Work such as that done by the medieval and post-medieval archaeologists, or the vernacular architects, might have been usefully applied to post-1750 sites. In the event, now that the sun seems to have set on industrial archaeology, what we are left with are some important preserved sites on which work can presumably be done in the future, and many more lost for ever, virtually or wholly unrecorded.

There has recently been an attempt to bring what was worth saving of industrial archaeology back into the fold. Just as the vernacular architects have slowly realised that buildings are part of the landscape and archaeologists have similarly seen individual monuments in a wider context, so at last the physical remains of the Industrial Revolution have been seen as part of an industrial landscape. In fact, most of the general accounts of landscape history in particular counties (*The Making of the Loamshire Landscape* etc) say something about the impact of industry; how much depends on which county is involved and the interests of the author, but Barrie Trinder is the first writer to have attempted a general account of *The Making of the Industrial Landscape*. If this book has the influence it deserves it may herald a new era in which landscape historians take proper account of the impact of the Industrial Revolution, and in which those interested in this period approach their subject in the same way as those concerned with evidence for earlier landscapes, rather than imagining that they are engaged in some completely separate activity.

The overall impact of all these developments is that few local historians now need reminding of the importance of physical evidence. Arguably, most amateur enthusiasts never did. Although in the last few years the most popular opening gambit for new visitors to a record office has probably been those mind-deadening words, 'We're looking up our family tree' (as though archivists are supposed to reach for some arboreal prefabrication ready to hand on the search-room shelves), older members of the profession will recall the days when people came into the office with questions like, 'I'd like to look at some old maps of our village', or 'I've found this old —— down the road and I'd like to know what it was used for'. For many, an interest in local history begins when they find something, an old building, unexplained earthworks, or just a hole in the ground, and want to know what it is or was. They assume their local library will be able to tell them and usually end up by being shown, possibly for the first time, large-scale Ordnance Survey maps spanning the last hundred years (p. 75). If those who begin in this way are told of other map sources and where to find them, their enthusiasm may develop into a full study of their local landscape. The alternative starting-point, which should lead to the same end-result, is for someone to be shown an old map and to see something which he did not know about, such as a water-mill, or a colliery tramway, or some odd-looking unidentified feature. It is a natural reaction to ask, 'I wonder if there's anything left of that' and to go and look at the spot on the ground. Twenty years ago that could have led to the discovery of an abandoned water-mill with its wheel and some machinery left inside; or the stone sleeper-blocks of an early nineteenth-century horse-operated railway; or, less fortunately, a superficial inspection of the ground might have left the investigator none the wiser. Today, after a period in which both the urban and the rural landscape have changed very rapidly and much evidence of past life has been removed for ever, there is less scope for discoveries of this kind (either the mill will have been swept away or it will have become a private house or heritage centre) but any work on landscape history must include an appreciation of the importance of both written and non-written evidence and of how each relates to the other.

This latter point applies with especial force to anything still masquerading under the banner of industrial archaeology. One of the many silly aspects of this pursuit was the misdirected energy spent investigating on the ground what was already known from Ordnance Survey maps. Thus people drove hundreds of miles taking pictures of derelict collieries. This contributed as much to our knowledge of the coal industry as half an hour spent photocopying old OS maps, i.e. establishing the existence and location of nineteenth-century collieries. Had some of the time been spent measuring headstocks or other structures the work might have been of some value, but it rarely reached this point. Since the publication of the second edition of the Ordnance Survey (p. 75), the English landscape has been recorded in great detail on contemporary maps. By all means go and visit these places to see how they have changed; or look at buildings of the period or landscapes that have survived relatively unaltered. This, however, is to use the landscape for illustration—a perfectly legitimate pursuit and one which has served to enhance many people's interest in the past—rather than studying it for evidence as one does for earlier periods in which there are no ready-made maps. Similarly, if you find some feature on the ground . which you wish to identify, start by looking at the map sources for the area. If whatever it is is the product of the last century or so, it may well be possible to identify it simply from a sequence of large-scale maps and establish that it is not as old as you thought, or as other people told you.

This sort of common sense, not notable amongst the wilder enthusiasts of industrial archaeology, can be rationalised thus. For any period of English history since the Roman invasion the historian has two main sources of evidence: that which is written, mostly on parchment or paper (to a small extent on stone or other material), and that which survives either on or beneath the ground. Whereas for periods prior to the Roman invasion, history must be written almost wholly from archaeological evidence (which sometimes leads to the mistaken idea that 'archaeology' is the study of early history, instead of a method of enquiry used by historians and prehistorians), from the first century onwards archaeology is one of several techniques used by historians (or, in practice, archaeological discoveries are so used, since the actual discovery is usually done by people called archaeologists). The development of archaeology during the present century, and parallel changes in the study of architectural history, have led to the use of physical evidence down to a later period than was considered worthwhile a century ago, because it has been realised that in some circumstances this evidence can supply information not available from documents. The extent to which historians draw on archaeological evidence diminishes as one approaches the present day, since documents become available and supply information much more easily and completely than archaeological evidence can. Thus we would know little about the way of life of the ruling class of Roman Britain had substantial remains of their homes not survived to be discovered, excavated and in some cases preserved over the last two centuries. In the case of their medieval counterparts, we know something of the houses they lived in from surviving documents, including a few illustrations, but our knowledge would again be much poorer had a number of castles not survived and been investigated. Even in the early modern period, for which records survive in greater quantity, it is still useful to be able to examine surviving great houses to determine how they were constructed or occupied. If all the remaining Victorian great houses were to disappear tomorrow (on the other hand), a valuable part of our national heritage would have been lost, but the study of nineteenth-century social history or building technology would not suffer greatly, since both subjects are studied principally from written (often by this date, printed) sources.

Down to what date archaeological evidence retains more than illustrative value will vary. Thus, surviving remains of Tutbury Castle are visually impressive and useful in studying medieval military architecture, but they do not contribute anything substantial to our knowledge of how the Duchy of Lancaster was administered, even though Tutbury was one of the centres of that administration. Instead, we look at the voluminous archives of the duchy. By contrast, had archaeologists not uncovered and interpreted the visually much less impressive remains of a large timber-framed hall belonging to the early medieval rulers of Northumbria at Yeavering, we would know far less about the social and economic organisation of that kingdom in the age of Beowulf, since few of its administrative or judicial records survive.

The case of industrial remains illustrates the equally important point that archaeological evidence is only of value when it has been made *available*. The same is true in a somewhat different way of much historial research (imagine studying the history of medieval central government without the published calendars or unpublished finding-aids available in the PRO) but whereas documents can be gathered into record offices and kept there until there is time to explore them, this is often not possible in the case of physical evidence. Excavation is a non-repeatable exercise and unless the results of the enquiry are published the information is lost for ever. Similarly, if an important building containing in its structure unique evidence is not systematically recorded before demolition that evidence will also be lost. One of the reasons why industrial archaeology has contributed little to mainstream historical studies is because of the general superiority of written over physical evidence in the period of the Industrial Revolution. The other reason is the dismal failure of those interested in physical evidence to make their material available in the same way as those studying earlier remains have done. Twenty years ago, a number of surviving pre-1850 blast furnaces were identified. Little is known of the design and con-struction of either late charcoal blast furnaces (c. 1660–1750) or early coke furnaces, since few contemporary drawings survive and written descriptions tend to concentrate on best-practice rather than typical sites. Thanks to the failure of industrial archaeologists ever to get beyond compiling checklists and taking indifferent snapshots we still know little of the design and construction of these furnaces. Where are the published measured drawings of Morley Park, Apedale or Moira, much less those that have been demolished in the meantime? Similarly, very considerable sums of public money have been devoted in the last decade to the conservation of sites associated with Sir Richard Arkwright, the pioneer of water-powered cotton spinning. Buildings at Cromford and elsewhere have been repre-sented as the eighteenth-century counterparts of medieval cathedrals. Whereas generations of students have applied themselves to recording great churches in drawings, photographs and published reports of investigations above or below ground, we still await the appearance of either an elevation or plan of Arkwright's first mill in any scholarly publication.

The local historian interested in industrial history should perhaps bear two things in mind. In general, most of the evidence will come from maps and documents and while it may be interesting to go out and look at old buildings, they will probably not add much to what is known about a particular industry. Secondly, in circumstances where physical evidence can supply some of the answers (and the two examples in the previous paragraph are good illustrations of documents not explaining everything) the evidence must be invest-igated with the same thoroughness as that for earlier periods and must be studied in close conjunction with conventional historical sources. It is nonsense to claim, as writers in *Industrial Archaeology* sometimes used to, that 'no documentary evidence' had been forthcoming for their newly discovered Victorian limestone quarry; at the very least there will be maps. The same is true of earlier periods in which the starting point of some investigation may be field evidence: it is essential to integrate the study of written evidence, especially maps, with what is found on the ground.

Local history on the ground

The previous chapters have said something about written sources and maps; what about the practical use of field evidence in local history? In some cases, the latter simply means using the published or unpublished findings of previous investigators. This is normally so with sites accessible only by excavation, since the conduct of this type of archaeological research on a large scale is now extremely expensive and highly skilled. During the 1970s large sums were applied to such research and in most parts of the country full-time staff were employed to excavate sites in advance of their destruction by developers. It is not clear in all cases what academic gains were achieved by employing archaeologists to destroy the sites more slowly beforehand, since the results of this unprecedented campaign of excavation have not yet been published in full, much less interpreted by historians. This area of public expenditure has now been severely curtailed and, again, one can by no means be certain that the loss to scholarship will be as great as that claimed by some of those formerly employed in the field.

It is possible that the sort of small-scale limited research excavation traditionally conducted by volunteers working under skilled direction at weekends or during the summer holidays will re-assert itself as a more cost-effective method of enquiry than the sort of work, especially in towns, with which we became familiar ten years ago. On the other hand, it remains the case, as textbooks have long emphasised, that unskilled amateurs should not interefere with areas of archaeological interest, whether statutorily protected or not. Local historians interested in the evolution of the landscape should obviously be aware of evidence derived from excavation, but preferably through using the results of other people's research rather than digging holes in the ground themselves. Some of the sources of this information have already been mentioned. The most important will probably be the annual journal of your county antiquarian society (p. 18), which remains the outlet for most excavation reports. This is obviously worth checking for any work done on sites in your area, while the library may have offprints of articles from the national journals relating to sites of more than local interest. Conversely, you may know of (or even have taken part in) excavations whose results appear not to have been published anywhere, in which case it may be worth pursuing notebooks, drawings or photographs in the hands of a local museum, library or record office, or contacting the excavator or his family.

Even if no excavations appear to have taken place in your parish, it is unlikely that there will have been no archaeological discoveries of any kind. Although excavation is the type of research that attracts most attention, there is a long tradition of fieldwork above ground in British archaeology, which is vastly cheaper to undertake and is the aspect of the subject which has fused with other types of field enquiry to become landscape history. This is the area in which the individual amateur can make the largest contribution, but before starting enquiries of one's own, it is as well to see what has already been discovered. Again, the main source of published information will be the county journal, other local publications and, perhaps most important, the archaeological chapters of VCH (pp. 20, 26). In many counties these will have been written before the first war and now seem badly out of date, but at least they provide a sound *resumé* of the state of knowledge at that time, collecting together and analysing references to discoveries from the seventeenth century onwards. Since these summaries were published, more sites have been found but only occasionally has later work been brought together in county-wide gazetteers, while in many cases finds remain unpublished. In some areas, local museums have long maintained card indexes of archaeological features, based on material brought to them or work by their own field officers. Alternatively, a county archaeological society may have done the same thing on a voluntary basis. When most counties acquired archaeological 'units' funded by the Department of the Environment in the 1970s, one of their functions was the compilation of what was usually christened 'the *sites and monuments record*'. This was another card index (in a few areas the data was stored in a computer from the start or later automated), bringing together earlier discoveries and adding the results of fieldwork by the unit. As the dust settles on the unpublished excavations of these organisations, it may well prove that the non-excavational fieldwork, often resulting in thousands of new finds, will be regarded as the most valuable side of their work. If you are interested in the landscape history of your parish, try to find out where the local sites and monuments record is (either at the unit itself, a local museum or a county planning department) and see what it has for your area.

One of the sources used by sites and monuments records was the material collected over a much longer period by the Archaeology Branch of the Ordnance Survey, which until recently maintained a national index of archaeological features. Material from this formed the basis of the 'period maps' published by the OS, such as that of Roman Britain, and the publication of 'antiquities' on modern OS maps of all scales, but far more features were included in the index than were ever published. If this material is not available locally, it is possible to obtain copies of the cards for your area from the Ordnance Survey. The OS index should not be confused with the National Monuments Record at the Ancient Monuments Branch of the Department of the Environment (Fortress House, 23 Savile Row, London W1). This used to be known as the National Buildings Record and is still predominantly a collection of drawings and photographs of buildings from all parts of England. Again, local investigators can obtain details of the NMR's holdings for a particular area; conversely, the NMR welcomes donation of photographs of buildings (not necessarily statutorily protected) submitted by local historians. In Wales copies of the OS cards and the NMR are both housed at the Royal Commission on Ancient and Historical Monuments for Wales (Edleston House, Queens Road, Aberystwyth, Dyfed).

Local historians interested in landscape history will probably also wish to get hold of *air photographs* of their area, which apart from being of considerable general interest can, under some circumstances, show up otherwise unknown archaeological features impossible to detect on the ground. Various official agencies have collections of air photographs, not all of which are readily accessible to the public. The DoE at Fortress House can supply details of these sources, while at local level it is often worth asking the county (or borough) surveyor's department if they can help. Even if the local authority is unwilling to supply spare prints free, it may give details of a recent commercial aerial survey of its territory and one can then approach the firm concerned. In Wales, the Conservation and Land Division of the Welsh Office is generally the best source of information about air photographs of the principality.

The Ordnance Survey period maps represent one kind of publication which can result from indexes of scattered finds or field monuments. The maps in the archaeological chapters of VCH were an earlier, more modest venture in the same direction. More recently, the ideal towards which many archaeologists have been working is the production of maps of a complete past landscape, getting away from the idea of a 'distribution map' or a map showing all the features of a certain kind set against a modern background, and striving to reconstruct a total picture. Few sites and monuments records are as yet sufficiently complete to allow this sort of reconstruction but where a county archaeological survey has been published this at least represents a new starting-point for more detailed local enquiries. At their best, for example in the volumes published for West Yorkshire, these surveys indicate the way in which 'landscape history' (alias 'total archaeology') is maturing. Few amateurs working part-time will have the resources to produce such elaborate maps as those accompanying the West Yorkshire survey, but that should not deter them from thinking along the same lines. At the very least, it should be possible to draw together archaeological discoveries, either by yourself or other people, into a series of simple 'period maps' for your own area. For the prehistoric and Roman periods, this will normally involve marking such discoveries on a base map containing only the natural features in the modern landscape. Although from time to time exponents of the idea of 'continuity' in the landscape have made extravagant claims for the extent to which Roman or even prehistoric features (e.g. territorial boundaries or fields) are embedded in much later landscapes, it is normally impossible to substantiate ideas of this kind. On the other hand, as indicated in the previous chapter (p. 91), the practised local historian should be able to recognise clues on large-scale nineteenth-century maps which suggest what the medieval landscape looked like, and to 'peel away' later features, working backwards towards Domesday Book.

How much the actual inspection of the landscape can contribute to post-Roman landscape history depends largely on what has happened to it in the much more recent past. The landscape may have been the most valuable historical document which Maitland's generation possessed, but he was writing at the end of the last century, before a revolution in British farming, a great extension of the built-up area, and large-scale opencast coalworking. Some more recent writers have also spoken in extravagant terms about the need to get mud on boots and the exhilaration of striding over a landscape barely changed since the days of Chaucer. To local historians in certain parts of the country this advice will have a hollow ring. Dating hedgerows by counting the number of species is hardly possible if most of the hedges have disappeared in the last thirty years in your district or the fields themselves have been completely changed by mining or quarrying. Many minor earthworks marked but not identified on the OS 25 inch plans of the 1880s have now gone for ever and their history can only be sought from other maps, field-names or documents. The same may well be true in your parish of one of the best known of all rural landscape features, the corrugated 'ridge and furrow' effect given to some open field arable in the middle ages by medieval ploughmen. Some very good examples of ridge and furrow survive in the Midlands and elsewhere and are regularly photographed for books and television programmes extolling the delights of history on the ground. Much more has been ploughed out, either recently by modern deep-ploughing, or over a longer period if the open fields disappeared in the fifteenth or sixteenth centuries and the land remained arable. Even in areas of parliamentary enclosure, it is often easier to map the open fields by careful redrawing of old maps or air photographs on modern base material than by surveying field evidence. Similarly, it is still possible to find ditches and banks on the ground which once marked the boundaries of medieval parks or even Anglo-Saxon estates, but there are many areas where evidence of this kind has all been swept away and can now only be recovered from looking closely at field boundaries and field-names recorded on the tithe map.

History on the ground will always be fun, and in some parts of the country there is still much to look at or even to find for the first time; but elsewhere the opportunities for this kind of fieldwork are more limited, and maps and documents a more fruitful source than the modern landscape. This is also the case with those bits of the landscape whose present owners or tenants have yet to be convinced of the attractions of landscape history and prefer not to have people tramping across their farms.

It was the Ordnance Survey map, rather than the landscape itself, that was once described as a marvellous palimpsest which we still do not fully understand. The OS maps of the late nineteenth century are still there to study; the landscape they portrayed, with all its clues to a much earlier period, has now been swept away in many areas. In a sense, of course, this simply bears out the claim that the landscape is an important historical source, but not in quite the same way as that statement is usually meant. If most of your parish is now covered with post-war housing estates or if most of the farmland has been affected by opencast coalworking then it remains true that the landscape reflects the history of the area. Unfortunately, the changes of recent decades have been so sweeping that the resulting landscape may contain only evidence of what has happened in the last thirty years, whereas in 1900 it might have been possible to look at features dating from every century since Anglo-Saxon times.

Buildings in the landscape

Until the end of the last century, and in many cases until well into this, local antiquaries took account of only two buildings in a parish, the Anglican church and the manor house. Even the great house, as opposed to its occupiers, only began to receive attention towards the end of the nineteenth century. One of the most important aspects of the post-war revolution in local studies has been the intense interest devoted to more modest domestic buildings (and in some areas, e.g. industrial South Wales, to non-Anglican places of worship also). A few students of 'folklife' or traditional building materials were already looking at local architectural styles before the war but over the last thirty years there have been a number of general and regional studies of vernacular architecture and more recently a journal has been established. The official bodies concerned with architectural history, such as the Ancient Monuments Branches of the Department of the Environment and the Welsh Office, and the Royal Commissions on Ancient and Historical Monuments for England and Wales have also paid much more attention to investigating small domestic buldings. Parallel with this, there has been a continuing interest in more traditional aspects of the subject, taking in the surviving secular buildings of the middle ages and the country houses of the sixteenth century and later. New areas have developed here also, such as an interest in landscape parks and gardens around great (or not so great) houses, or a new enthusiasm for Victorian and Edwardian buildings, rural and urban. Nineteenth-century working-class housing has also attracted attention for the first time.

These changes have affected the study of local communities in various ways, apart from the quite different but equally important shift in our view of what should be preserved from the past. Perhaps above all, buildings, polite as well as vernacular, are now seen as 'documents' supplying important historical evidence and not merely as illustrations of a bygone age. Like all source material, they will only yield useful information if studied intelligently. In the case of vernacular buildings, both urban and rural, a systematic procedure was evolved for their study in the 1950s at the school of architecture at Manchester University, which has been simplified for wider consumption and is fully explained in R. W. Brunskill's *Ilustrated Handbook of Vernacular Architecture*. The system involves isolating the component parts of a small or medium-sized domestic building (roof, walls, doors, windows, chimney stacks and so on); the style or position of these features within the building (e.g. hipped roof, lateral chimney stack, central doorway); and the materials of which each component is built (this includes distinguishing, for example, different brickwork bonds or methods of stonemasonry). Finally, the position of the building in relation to other buildings, especially farm buildings, and its general alignment are noted. There are always risks in reducing any fieldwork to the ticking of boxes on record cards but the Manchester system has many attractions. It is comprehensive and well worked out; it can be applied to any part of the country and to both urban and rural building. The information required for the survey can normally be obtained from an external inspection of the building and can be collected quite quickly without measuring or surveying. Above all, by asking detailed questions about every aspect of a building, it forces the observer to look very closely at its salient features.

The Manchester system of recording vernacular building was intended to provide a rapid but reasonably detailed summary record of local styles and materials across fairly large regions (ultimately, it was hoped, the whole country) that could be followed up by a more detailed examination of typical or particularly interesting buildings. A few regional studies of this kind were completed at Manchester in the 1950s and later, combining widespread summary examination of the domestic architecture of a district with measured drawings of selected buildings. This work was concentrated mainly in rural areas, but during the same period the Leicester Local History Department became the home of several urban studies, which tend to present problems not susceptible to summary analysis because of the greater degree of change in towns. Here the approach was a very full, virtually house-by-house survey involving large numbers of measured drawings and a close study of documents. More recently, both the English and Welsh Royal Commissions have issued substantial volumes on vernacular housing, drawing on examples studied by their staff in advance of demolition. Besides these studies, numerous individual buildings, or particular methods of construction or materials, have been the subject of articles either in *Vernacular Architecture* or the archaeological journals.

For the local historian interested in old buildings there is thus a large general literature on what has already been discovered and how such buildings should be studied. In most parts of England there remains much scope for the amateur fieldworker, although in Wales, where the Royal Commission has less ground to cover and where other bodies such as the Welsh Folk Museum have also been active, there is probably rather less. In some parts of the country, a simple summary survey as described by Brunskill would be useful; elsewhere, the basic features of the vernacular tradition are now fairly well established, although more detailed surveys, with measured drawings of particular houses, may not have been done. Closer examination of buildings from the inside as well as outside may also reveal a more complicated history than was apparent during a summary survey. This is almost always the case in towns where there is also more chance of supplementing field evidence with that of documents, such as deeds, rentals or other estate records, or probate inventories (pp. 54, 63). Apart from inventories, this material is less plentiful for cottages and farmhouses in the countryside.

For every county in England there is now a published volume in the 'Buildings of England' series compiled by Sir Nikolaus Pevsner and his collaborators, a series that is also being extended to Wales. These gazetteers do not normally contain detailed descriptions of many vernacular buildings but are useful for churches and the larger domestic buildings, and also for their lengthy introductions on the building history of a county in general. Probably more useful for the local historian working on a particular parish will be the unpublished but accessible 'Lists of Buildings of Special Architectural or Historic Interest', including buildings 'listed' by the Department of the Environment or Welsh Office as being worthy of protection. Local libraries or planning departments should have copies of the lists for their areas, which are usually short enough to have photocopied at no great expense. They are a good starting point for a local survey, although some of the older lists were compiled very rapidly and did not take full account of vernacular buildings now considered worth listing. More recent lists are much fuller but are still based — inevitably, given the amount of ground the staff have to cover—on a fairly brief external examination of the buildings, which a local investigator should be able to amplify considerably. The departments responsible for listing welcome suggestions for new additions to the list or corrections to the existing descriptions of buildings already listed.

Some readers interested in old buildings may simply wish to establish the date of their own home. For them, sources mentioned in this chapter and in that on maps, as well as the relevant section of Chapter 3 (pp. 54–61) should provide a fairly full guide; because of the popularity of 'tracing the history of your house' there are now several booklets which cover this topic in detail.

As with any specialised field, many of those interested in vernacular architecture seem to regard the study of old buildings as an end in itself and have shown little interest in the evidence the buildings provide even for the history of technology, much less for more general social and economic history. On a broader level, however, a model has been devised to account for the survival of the corpus of buildings that forms the raw material in this field. On the one hand, vernacular architecture is concerned with the study of buildings made of locally available materials and built according to local rather than national (or 'polite') ideas of design. There is thus a 'vernacular threshold' which moves over time and progressively excludes a larger proportion of the total housing stock. Medieval great houses, including castles, were not 'vernacular', nor by the seventeenth or eighteenth century were many more modest town and country houses. In the second half of the nineteenth century, the distribution by rail of cheap mass-produced building materials brought an end to the use of local materials, first in towns and then in the countryside, so that by 1900 even the most modest working class houses had ceased to be vernacular. Another feature of the housing stock in the past which limits the material available for study is the permanence of the structure. Medieval great houses were built to last and many have done so to the present day; medieval peasant houses were not and do not normally survive. During the period character- ised as the 'Great Rebuilding' (roughly 1540 to 1700 but varying between different regions) the majority of the population came to live, for the first time, in permanent houses, of which again large numbers have survived to this day. Only in the eighteenth or even nineteenth century did the poorest inhabitants of the poorest regions of the north and west live in such houses. The overall effect of these two forces—the vernacular threshold and permanence of structure —means that the subject has tended to be concerned most with the early modern period, plus some larger houses which have survived from the middle ages and smaller cottages of a rather later period. It is not concerned either with medieval great houses or with nineteenth-century 'bye-law' housing, neither of which was ver- nacular, nor with medieval peasant houses, which have to be excavated.

The local historian seeking to use the evidence of vernacular architecture in a study of his community, rather than being merely interested in surveying old buildings, should be able to apply this model to what he sees around him. The impermanence of medieval cottages and the general renewal of the housing stock in the sixteenth and seventeenth centuries are now well established concepts, but it is also important to look for other upswings in the building cycle since the Great Rebuilding. In some areas there was little or no compre- hensive rebuilding after 1700 until recent years, so that in much of lowland southern England it was possible, until the extensive changes wrought to the rural housing stock in the last ten or fifteen years, to see evidence for the Great Rebuilding in every village. In other parts of the country, however, comparatively little survives from this period because of later alterations. In particular, the extensive renewal of farmhouses and farm buildings that seems to have taken place in regions benefiting from the prosperous farming of the Napoleonic War years (1793–1815) may have swept away most or all older building. This is just as much a 'Great Rebuilding' as the better known one two hundred years earlier, and for most parts of the country can best be appreciated by looking at surviving farmhouses, since documentary evidence at local level is often limited. Alternatively, the farms and houses in a village may all date from the late nineteenth century and may all have been built by a single owner, often in a distinctive, uniform and not necessarily vernacular style. This too may be historical evidence not preserved anywhere else, if the estate in question has no surviving muniments.

Endless study of different kinds of dovetails or chamfers may fascinate students of vernacular architecture, but for the material to be of wider value it must be seen in a broader context. Housing is a form of expenditure, one to which most people accord a high priority. If they are well off they will spend more money on better housing; if they are poor they will make their existing housing last longer. The date of most of the surviving houses in your village is therefore a guide to its changing prosperity since the appearance of permanent housing for the majority of the people in the sixteenth century. To use this evidence you must first work out the date of the housing stock and then see how this evidence relates to that from other sources. If there is little sign of change between the Great Rebuilding and the coming of the M4 to within ten miles of the village then that is evidence for a lack of prosperity between about 1700 and 1970, of the village having been unaffected by parliamentary enclosure, the Industrial Revolution, the Napoleonic War, High Farming or the Town and Country Planning Acts. If, by contrast, your village has virtually no building surviving from before 1800 and most of the farms are square Georgian brick boxes then the village may have been transformed by the first three of these factors. If half the cottages of the parish have changed little since the Great Rebuilding but the other half all seem to have been done up about 1900 and have the same person's initials on them, that is evidence that one of the two estates decided its tenants needed better housing and perhaps employed a minor Arts and Crafts movement architect to restore the property. Changes of this kind may be traceable only from visual evidence; alternatively, such evidence may lead to a search for documents which confirm or refute an idea. If, for example, your parish contains a secondary settlement made up of rather poor early nineteenth-century cottages it is worth looking at maps to see whether they were built on a piece of common waste by people unable to get houses in the main village. If all the villages in your area have a neat row of post-war council houses near their edge it may be worth searching out the minutes of the rural district council's housing committee (p. 53) to see why the authority decided to build them.

Urban housing should be looked at in the same way, although with older structures there may be considerable technical problems of interpretation if the building has been extensively and repeatedly altered. The basic idea is the same, however: the age-profile of the housing of a community is an index of its wealth over time, combined with the impact of public or private individuals or corporations on the supply of land for building or the supply of buildings themselves. Thus, if your town was greatly enlarged (or even built from scratch) around the end of the twelfth century it was because (a) that was a period of rapid economic growth, and (b) the lord of the manor decided to develop his estate by enlarging or building a town. If your town centre was completely rebuilt in the 1960s then (as you will probably remember) the first of those explanations still applies, except that for 'lord of the manor' one substitutes 'property developer' or 'local authority'. Less dramatic change to individual buildings or streets can be explained in the same way. At its simplest, one can date streets added to the town in the nineteenth century, either by looking at the housing on them or by looking at maps and documents (pp. 72, 54). On streets that have been built up since the middle ages there will typically be a mixture of property, perhaps including a house that actually incorporates interesting late medieval structure, but it is the age of the bulk of the property that is important in using physical evidence for more general local history. The present appearance of High Street, Burford, should not just be drooled over but seen partly as a reflection of the late medieval and early modern wealth of this important centre of the Cotswold wool trade; and equally, as (a) a reflection of the relative decline of the town in the period 1700–1900, from which there is little building, and (b) the wealth of the town since 1945, which accounts for the careful conservation of High Street today. The latter is also a reflection of modern views of what one does with sixteenth- and seventeenth-century houses, whereas had Burford become the home of some major nineteenth-century industry most of that housing would have been demolished as old-fashioned and insanitary.

Local historians often belong to conservation or amenity societies and, when such activities were more popular than they are today, did much to campaign against the destruction of old buildings. They should not, however, succumb to the temptation to see an attractive row of cottages or town houses merely as evidence that their community is 'old' or 'historic' or 'ancient'. Buildings are evidence, just like documents and the landscape. They are of course useful evidence for students of building technology but they may also supply information about the past economy of a community which is obtainable from no other source—or they may at least illustrate aspects of economic and political history which are studied principally from written sources. Local historians should look past the next base-cruck and try to work out why a family had the money to put a new double wind-braced through-purlin roof on its house.

Chapter six
THE PUBLIC RECORD OFFICE & OTHER NATIONAL COLLECTIONS

Since this book is aimed at the beginner, it may seem wrong to include a chapter on a repository which is undoubtedly not the place to *start* local history research and which is not greatly used by amateurs at all. On the other hand, all local historians come across references to the Public Record Office and most are interested in knowing what it is and what its holdings consist of. The PRO itself issues a leaflet on local history, and the older textbooks, especially Cox's *How to Write the History of a Parish*, dwell heavily on centrally preserved sources. One reason, of course, why most local historians make limited use of the PRO is that the average amateur enthusiast living in the provinces, especially one with a regular job outside education, only occasionally has the chance to visit London during the working day. Even local historians within a tube journey of Chancery Lane may well have to fit trips to the PRO into annual leave, so for this reason alone it is worth giving some advice to help make visits as effective as possible. This chapter also mentions some of the other national libraries and record repositories which the local historian may use.

The Public Record Office

As explained earlier (p. 19), the PRO was established in 1838 to provide a single home for the judicial and administrative records of central government which had previously been kept in the Tower of London and elsewhere, mostly in unsatisfactory conditions. Into it were gathered the records of the two great institutions of medieval administration, the Chancery and the Exchequer, the records of the central judiciary, and those of several minor courts. As the nineteenth-century revolution in government progressed, so the volume of archives increased and more recent material was transferred to the PRO from an increasing number of departments. The office was originally housed in a building near the southern end of Chancery Lane but in modern times records have been stored on several other sites. Today, the PRO operates from four premises, including a repository at Hayes in west London, not open to the public, where recent government files are kept. The three branches of the office used by readers are the building at Chancery Lane; accommodation nearby at Portugal Street where the census enumerators' books are produced on microfilm; and the record office at Kew, which houses modern archives and was once intended to become the department's main home. In simple terms, the records of medieval central government and of the law courts down to modern times are kept at Chancery Lane, those of modern departments of state at Kew. The PRO issues a list of exactly which classes are where and for the local historian there is much of interest at both Chancery Lane and Kew. The census is not described here, since most local historians will have discovered this material on microfilm at their local library or record office (p. 34) and will not need to travel to London to search the material in the rather gloomy and very crowded surroundings of Portugal Street.

If the holdings of a county record office can seem overwhelming on a first visit, then the contents of the PRO, covering as they do almost every department of one of the most sophisticated, highly centralised governments in the world, are bound to be much more difficult to grasp. Even the vast range of published work on the contents of the PRO, ranging from complete transcripts of certain key documents, through calendars of the main administrative records of medieval government, to simple lists of modern material, takes some time to get to know thoroughly. The best starting point is still the three volume *Guide to the Contents of the Public Record Office* published by HMSO in the 1960s, although one volume of this is now out of print and the whole set is being replaced by a guide stored in a computer which can be updated at will. Even more than with a local office, it is essential to read as much as possible about the PRO before you set foot in the building, so as to understand what you will find and how to make best use of your time there.

The PRO *Guide* is useful in the first place in explaining in more detail what is at Chancery Lane and what is at Kew. With a few exceptions, material described in Volume I is at Chancery Lane, that in Volume II at Kew. Volume III describes records transferred to the office after the publication of the first two books; where these are additions to existing groups they have obviously gone with the older archives of the same department, while most of the new groups are at Kew. Secondly, the *Guide* is the only thorough introduction to the contents of the office as a whole. Records at the PRO are divided into 'groups', each of which is divided into one or more 'classes', while each class consists of a number (often a very large number) of 'pieces', each of which has an individual reference number. Understanding this threefold arrangement is a good start towards unravelling the complexities of central government archives. A 'group' in the PRO normally means the records of a particular court (Chancery, Exchequer, Common Pleas, etc at Chancery Lane) or department (Home Office, Foreign Office, Treasury, etc at Kew). The subdivision into classes varies according to the nature of each department's work and is impossible to summarise. Each group in the published *Guide* has a simple mnemonic reference (C for Chancery, HO for Home Office, etc); recent accessions have for some reason been given group letters with no intrinsic meaning. Each class is given a number and a brief description in the *Guide*. Thus, to take a couple of examples used a good deal by local historians, PROB 11 are the registered copy wills of the Prerogative Court of Canterbury, which form one class within the PCC group; E179 are lay subsidies and other tax returns preserved among the very extensive records of the Exchequer.

The PRO *Guide* describes every class that was in the office when the book was published but it does not list the pieces within each class whose numbers you need to order the documents to the search-room. For this you need a 'class list', which is where the jungle of PRO finding-aids becomes more complicated. Every class a local historian is likely to want to use is listed but not all the lists have been published, and those that have do not form a single series. For some classes the *Guide* lists what published finding-aids there are (transcripts, calendars or descriptive lists) and these can normally be found in a large reference library or university library; they are catalogued in a free booklet issued by HMSO. The oldest publications are those of the early nineteenth-century Record Commission, which are generally full transcripts of basic medieval sources, such as Henry VIII's survey of church wealth of 1535, *Valor Ecclesiasticus*, the book referred to on p. 30 as one whose title is often incomprehensibly abbreviated because it is so well known. In a slightly different category are the long series of calendars (bound in dark green cloth) published by the PRO since the late nineteenth century, providing detailed summaries in English of the main administrative records of the medieval Chancery and a few other classes. These form the *Cal.* family who also turn up, to the bafflement of beginners, in the footnotes to scholarly works (*Cal.Pat.R.*, *Cal.Cl.R.*, *Cal.Ch.R.*, etc) and are explained in the *Guide*. Thirdly, the PRO issued in the past a series of *Lists and Indexes*, supplying piece numbers for certain classes. These are the converse of the relevant section of the *Guide*: they say nothing about what the documents contain but give full reference numbers for ordering items in the search-room.

While the existence of calendars and lists is indicated in the *Guide*, nothing is said there (because the series had not then been inaugurated) about a newer set of publications, those of the List & Index Society, which was established by PRO users to reproduce unpublished finding aids kept only on the search-room shelves, and to distribute them to subscribing libraries. This series, which can be recognised from some distance by its unattractive green and yellow binding, simply prints whatever is available at the PRO for a particular class, usually a typed list with manuscript amendments. Because the series was set up by record users it has concentrated on heavily used classes where the lack of a published list was proving frustrating to searchers outside London, and many of these are of local interest. Like the older finding aids, the series is available in university and larger public libraries.

As with a local record office, only more so, it is essential to go to the PRO with some idea of what you want to see, if possible with exact references to three documents (the most that will be produced at once) with which to get started. Often, one can pick up an initial reference from a footnote in a printed book, although there is no point going to the PRO to check a medieval reference if you will not be able to read the document, or just to check whether the editor of the relevant volume of the *Calendar of Patent Rolls* has got all the details right (he almost certainly will, and in any case patent rolls are not easy to read). Similarly, although the PRO staff are very good at answering letters, there is no general index of personal and place-names at the office from which they can identify all the references to your village or family, and the staff can certainly not undertake genealogical searches for you. It is unproductive to turn up at the PRO just to see what they have got on your parish without having some idea where to look, or to arrive with the name of an ancestor hoping to find a series of references to him in some huge index.

It is obviously impossible in a book such as this to describe, or even list, all the classes in the PRO which contain material of local interest. I have simply referred to a few categories of central government records which are fairly easy to read, have not been included in published calendars, and will yield information about local communities. This includes some genealogical material, although a recent PRO publication covers this ground more thoroughly. First, however, a word about the mechanics of getting into the PRO.

It is usually best to write to the office before a first visit, either simply asking for an application form for a reader's ticket or asking some fairly precise question about documents you are interested in, plus details of how to come and look at them. In either case, you will be sent various introductory leaflets and an application form. If you find yourself in central London with several hours to spare and a couple of definite references it may be worth presenting yourself at Chancery Lane with some means of identification, filling in an application form on the spot and going straight into the office. People tend not to find themselves in Ruskin Avenue, Kew, in similar circumstances. If possible, however, get a ticket first, then identify some documents to start on, then visit the office, having established which branch—Chancery Lane or Kew—your material is in. The older part of the office is easy enough to get to, and the

PRO issues a leaflet explaining how to find Kew. Despite its unpopularity with some academic users for whom outer west London is a strange country and the motor car an alien form of transport, Kew has the great advantages of lying just off the South Circular Road near the start of the M4 and of having a large free car park. There is no public parking at Chancery Lane. The system for ordering documents at both Kew and Chancery Lane is automated: whereas one used to fill in duplicate requisition slips by hand, readers at both branches now type the same information into a computer. This saves the staff having to enter the details at the end of the day from the slips (which they do to see which documents are in demand from whom), but the computer does not actually go and get the boxes from the strong-room; there will be some delay (its length fluctuates considerably) in the production of material. At Chancery Lane, where the production of documents takes longer because of the arrangement of the stacks, one can order three items in advance by phone or letter. To do this you must have a reader's ticket (since its number must be quoted) but the system avoids perhaps an hour's wait when you arrive (the office opens at 9.30) before you have anything to look at.

The ground rules for working at the PRO apply to both main branches and are similar to those in most county offices. You may not take briefcases, sandwiches or the like into the search-rooms; notes must be taken in pencil; and you may only have three documents out at once. At both branches, orders are not accepted after 3.30 p.m. and so it is important to have a steady supply of references to hand to maintain a flow of documents throughout the day. As soon as your first three arrive you may order another three, and so on. Both at Chancery Lane and Kew typewriters may be used without seeking permission in advance; at Kew there is no objection to the use of small cassette recorders and an ample supply of power sockets for electric typewriters. For most of the material at Chancery Lane, however, a pencil and paper is still the best method of making notes. At both Chancery Lane and Kew there is a photocopying service, which is extremely expensive and, for most types of copy, very slow. If you wish to look at a single document and you live in Cumberland it is more economical to order a photocopy than make a visit, but large-scale copying at the PRO is for most people prohibitively expensive. In the specific case of census microfilm try to find some means of making hard copy off locally held film, rather than ordering prints from the PRO. In every case, get a firm estimate from the office (which will demand payment in advance) and explain very clearly what you want to have copied and by what method.

Because it is a more modern building and most of its holdings are straightforward volumes and files, the Kew branch of the PRO is probably a simpler place to work than Chancery Lane. At Kew the main public area consists of a reference room, which contains vast members of index volumes, lists and other finding-aids, and a large, comfortable search-room. If you arrive knowing which class you wish to search for local references, ask a member of staff to show you the list for that class, note the numbers of pieces you are interested in, and type the first three into the computer, which itself dispenses advice on how to order documents. At Chancery Lane there is a reference room with similar finding-aids but the class-lists from which you identify call-numbers are kept on the shelves of the two main search-rooms, the Round Room and Long Room. Two smaller rooms on the first floor are intended for people reading PCC wills and other probate material or maps. Readers are not allowed to commute between search-rooms reading three documents in each simultaneously (although you can go and look at wills while you are waiting for documents to arrive downstairs), nor, except with special permission, can documents produced in one room be taken to another. It is therefore necessary, unless you are merely looking at wills or maps, to choose one of the downstairs rooms as your base for the day. Typewriters can only be used in the Long Room, which for most other readers is a good reason for using the Round Room, which also has more comfortable seats and most of the finding aids for the older records. If you order documents in advance you will be asked to specify the room to which you wish them to be brought.

The local historian arriving at Chancery Lane for the first time will almost certainly be struck by the grandeur of the building (especially the impressive interior of the Round Room), which can now be appreciated properly after recent restoration, and at the same time confused by the huge number of calendars, lists and indexes all around him in both the Round Room and Long Room. The antidote to feeling overwhelmed is to think small to begin with: do not attempt a frontal assault on the entire records of the medieval Chancery or Exchequer but come with the name of a class you wish to check for your parish or, better still, three specific references. Best of all, be able to walk into one of the search-rooms and find three documents waiting for you at the counter. If you do feel completely lost, or cannot grasp the way in which the finding aids work, ask for help. Here, as elsewhere in the civil service, much depends on knowing whom to ask. The counter staff are there to control the flow of material between strong-room and search-room; they may be questioned about unexplained delays in the production of documents but not about how to trace the history of your village. That sort of enquiry (preferably in a more specific form) is ideally directed to the officer in charge of the Round Room, who sits on the left of the room as you go in. Although his desk is raised up above those of readers, the main function of an assistant keeper of public records on duty in the Round Room is not to make sure that people are not using felt-tip pens or surreptitiously munching sandwiches, nor to deal with the files on his desk. He (or she) is there to field readers' enquiries, whether they are about twelfth-century or twentieth-century records, and regardless of whom they come from. The staff cannot give more than occasional advice on actually reading the documents, and so it is as well not to order material likely to be written in a hand or language in which you have not had some practice in a local office. This reservation apart, however, the professional staff, especially the assistant keepers, are a mine of information and invariably helpful. As at Kew, the best way to start at Chancery Lane is to know which class you are interested in and then ask the staff where the class list is to be found. You will probably be shown at the same time the card index by the door of the Round Room, which identifies the position on the Round Room and Long Room shelves of the list for every class in the *Guide*.

After this preamble on how to use the place, something should now be said on what to look at at the PRO. As with a local record office, this depends to some extent on what subject you are pursuing, but let us take the simple case of someone generally interested in the history of his town or village. Leaving on one side the medieval public records (since the administrative material is mostly accessible in print and the judicial sources beyond most amateurs), there are a number of classes at Chancery Lane for the period 1500–1700 which are well within the grasp of anyone with some practice in reading secretary hand.

If you have no specific leads to follow, a good class to start with may be E179, which contains tax returns from the beginning of the fourteenth century to the end of the seventeenth. The documents are arranged by county and within each county by date. There is a list published by the List and Index Society. Assuming the material has not been printed for your county by a local record society, it is usually worth looking at hearth tax assessments for your parish, since these should provide a fairly complete list of householders for at least one date during the period 1662–88 when the tax was collected. There will be a separate assessment for each hundred within the county, so order the piece for the hundred in which your parish lies. For each parish there will be a list of names of those who paid hearth tax, possibly followed by a list of those who were exempt on the grounds of poverty, plus the number of hearths each householder had in his house. The latter is a rough guide to social standing, and in villages where there was only one large house it should be possible to identify the occupier from the tax assessment. Names in hearth tax lists can also be linked to probate records, to see whether people with large houses have large inventories. A hearth tax assessment which includes those discharged from payment as well as those charged should include almost every household in the parish. Multiply the number of names by 4.75 and you have a rough estimate of population to compare with that for 1801 from the first census.

Hearth tax records come right at the end of E179 and it will probably be worthwhile going back over the previous hundred years of the class to look at other tax returns. Most of these will be assessments to lay subsidies, a tax (to which the clergy were assessed separately, hence the name) levied on men's wealth in goods or land. In the second half of the sixteenth century its imposition became fossilised and fell very lightly on only a few people in each village (sometimes called 'subsidymen' as a mark of social standing), but two subsidies of the reign of Henry VIII are rich sources for the local historian. For southern English counties that of 1524–7 should provide a list of householders in each community, excluding the poorest third of the population who were exempt from the tax. For northern England and Wales (which was only brought into the English tax system in 1536) the subsidy of 1543–7 is likely to be fuller. Tax returns of this period are harder to read than hearth tax assessments, but anyone with experience of an early parish register should be able to read a simple list of names and amounts paid. For both lay subsidies and hearth tax, and indeed other contemporary material on population and social structure, there is a large literature on the documents and their exploitation.

The Tudor and Stuart Exchequer was not merely a revenue-collecting department but also a court of law, with a jurisdiction that brought before it many cases of local interest. During this period the Exchequer collected a great deal of evidence in 'depositions', which recorded witnesses' (strictly speaking, deponents') answers to a set of questions put before them by both plaintiff and defendant. These depositions are to be found mainly in two classes (E134 and E178) and abound in colourful local detail. The only published list appeared in the nineteenth century and was arranged chronologic-ally for the whole country. Many years ago, someone at the PRO had the good idea of cutting up a copy of this list and putting it back together again county-by-county; no-one has since had the even better idea of publishing these volumes. However, once you have found this pasted-up compilation on the Round Room shelves and looked up your county, the chances are there will be at least a couple of cases relating to people or places you are interested in. Documents in both E134 and E178 are written in English in a hand no more difficult than that used for local records of the same period. For each case there will usually be a file of several membranes of parchment, starting with a list of questions ('interrogatories') administered by plaintiff to his deponents. Then will come the answers, followed by the same sequence for the defendant. Both questions and answers are informal in style and often contain much topographical detail (descriptions of property or boundaries of manors), eye-witness accounts of disputed incidents (riotous assembly or illegal en-closure), and sometimes even reported speech (each side accusing the other of making incriminating statements). Depositions can also be a useful source of biographical information, since each witness prefaced his replies by giving his name, place of residence, occupation and age.

Depositions were a preliminary stage in an Exchequer action and it is sometimes possible to trace other documents in the case, following the directions given at the front of the Round Room list of depositions. Proceedings in other courts in the early modern period follow roughly the same course as in the Exchequer. Those for the Chancery are probably most accessible since there are published lists for cases from the middle of the sixteenth century to the middle of the seventeenth. Chancery depositions, however, are not as full as those taken by the Exchequer, although they are also in English rather than Latin.

The PRO contains large quantities of material generated by crown ownership of manors and other property, the equivalent of family and estate collections in local offices. Manorial documents are included in the National Register of Archives Register of Manorial Documents (p. 54) and so this source can be checked without difficulty. Court rolls and some cognate material, such as rentals and surveys, were brought together in the past in a group called Special Collections, which is well covered in the old series of *Lists and Indexes*. Elsewhere in Part I of the *Guide* will be found details of crown muniments for estates owned by the Duchy of Lancaster or the palatinates of Chester and Durham, which will be of value to local historians in certain parts of the country. The records of the Duchy of Cornwall remain in the hands of that body. For all parts of the country it is worth investigating those classes of Exchequer records which once belonged to the Court of Augmentations, set up by Henry VIII to administer confiscated monastic lands. While the wealth of the church on the eve of the Dissolution can be studied in the published *Valor Ecclesiasticus* mentioned earlier, the later history of former monastic lands and their disposal by Henry's successors has to be sought from the unprinted Augmentations records, unless a local society has published the material. There is a short account of Augmentations records in the *Guide*, and on the Round Room shelves there are a number of calendars of leases and grants of the lands which may make sending for the original deeds unnecessary, and may trace the history of an estate in your parish from the 1530s to the mid-seventeenth century. Augmentations records also contain material relating to the religious gilds and chantries dissolved by Edward VI, again including leases and grants tracing the later ownership of the property, most of which lay in towns. Finally, the Court of Augmentations, and other medieval departments of state, acquired large quantitites of deeds for property which passed through crown hands. The List and Index Society has issued calendars of thousands of these 'ancient deeds', supplementing older publications by the PRO itself, which are obviously worth checking for references to places in which you are interested.

These references by no means exhaust sources of local interest at Chancery Lane, but should provide the beginner with some leads from which to progress. The other main object of visits to Chancery Lane by local historians is to use the probate records of the Prerogative Court of Canterbury; these are produced in two adjacent first-floor search-rooms, where relevant finding-aids are kept on open access. The working of the church probate courts in England and Wales before 1858 has already been outlined (p. 62), and the position of the PCC at the head of the system explained. Wills from all parts of the country were proved in PCC where the estate was scattered, extensive or likely to prove complicated for the next of kin, although it was resorted to far more commonly by executors living in London and the south-east than those from more remote parts of the country. The best known PCC records are the volumes into which wills proved in the court were copied, which are now produced on microfilm and from which photocopies can be made, by PRO standards, quite quickly and cheaply. Indexes to grants from the beginning of the court's records (nominally 1383, although they do not start in bulk until the mid-sixteenth century) to 1700 have been published and are available in most major reference libraries. These can be used to identify wills of likely interest prior to a visit to the PRO, or to order photocopies. Between 1700 and 1750 and 1800 to 1857 searchers are dependent on manuscript indexes available only at the PRO, while for the intervening fifty years an index is now in process of publication by the Society of Genealogists.

The records of the PCC also include several thousand inventories, mainly for the period 1660–1760, which have now been cleaned, sorted and listed after years of neglect. Several lists have now been published in full by the List and Index Society. Far fewer PCC grants have surviving inventories compared with those from most local courts. The thorough exploration which PCC records have received in recent years has led to lists being compiled of a number of other classes, mainly to do with litigation in the court, whose existence was barely known before, and it is worth browsing through the newly compiled aids on the search-room shelves of the Wills Room. Except perhaps for a large parish near London, there will not be many PCC wills, administrations or inventories for a single community, but what there is will probably be of disproportionate interest compared with the records of the local court. The inventories may include one of a local country house, perhaps with the library or pictures listed in detail, and the wills will almost always be for people of some substance.

Sources for local history at the Kew branch of the Public Record Office are rather more homogeneous, like the material itself, than at Chancery Lane. Essentially, Kew has those records of the modern departments of state selected for permanent preservation, with some series starting in the seventeenth century, some in the eighteenth, but most in the nineteenth or twentieth. Large areas of Kew's most heavily used holdings, such as Cabinet, Foreign Office or Colonial Office records, or the service departments, contain nothing of local interest (although Navy and Army records can be useful for the history of towns with military connections). Some of the records of the more strictly domestic departments contain references to local communities, such as correspondence regarding early nineteenth-century 'disturbances' among the Home Office papers, or the files of dissolved companies transferred from the Board of Trade, but they are not arranged, or even indexed, by place. Kew is also the present home of the former British Transport Commission archives, consisting mainly of railway and canal company records, which are of interest to local historians but, as explained earlier (p. 71), have been heavily exploited by transport enthusiasts. For the local historian interested in discovering more about his parish generally, the material at Kew likely to be of greatest interest are the records of the nineteenth-century departments which supervised the creation of the modern system of local government, whose own records have already been described (pp. 48–54).

Each of the statutory reforms outlined in Chapter 3 involved the setting up of a central government department to supervise local elected boards. The pattern established by the Poor Law Amendment Act of 1834 was copied in the Public Health Acts of 1848 and later, and the Education Acts of 1870 and 1902. The records of the central department in each case include correspondence with each local authority in the earlier nineteenth century and, for the later period, files containing minutes (in the modern civil service sense) as well as letters to and from the authority. This material greatly amplifies what can be discovered of local government in a particular parish, including not merely public health reform but also poor relief and education. Even if the board of guardians or the local board has surviving letter-books containing correspondence with the Poor Law Board or Local Government Board it is useful to go to Kew and look at the central department's files as well, since they may contain comments by civil servants about policy, endorsed on letters from the local authority, and minutes to guide those responsible for drafting replies.

The records of the various ancestors of the Department of Education and Science—the Education Department of the Privy Council, the Board of Education and the Ministry of Education—are particularly useful for the local history of the subject from 1870 onwards. Not merely is there a series of files for each local authority (each school board under the 1870 Act, each county education committee or 'Part III' authority under that of 1902) but an even larger class containing a file for every school that has ever received a grant from central funds, in other words all schools in the maintained sector. This is one area where the modern records of central government reach down to the lowest level, adding to whatever is available in a county record office or at the school itself. These files, and those of the department's dealings with local authorities, are especially interesting where there was any clash, either between rival local interests, or between the local authority and the central department.

The Kew branch of the PRO has most of the maps preserved among the public records, since the main sources of English material are the two service departments and (perhaps unexpectedly) the Inland Revenue, which is the successor of the Tithe Commission and has transferred the central government copies of the tithe maps to the PRO, although it is normally simpler to look at a locally held copy of the award (p. 79).

From this very brief outline of material in the PRO of interest to local historians, or better still from the *Guide*, it should be possible to see how the records of central government relate to those in local record offices and how the two together, for different periods, are more or less useful for local studies. In simple terms, one can divide English history between the Norman Conquest and the first world war into three main periods, each of which has been marked by an increase in record creation and preservation as the machinery of government became more complex. Thus in the twelfth and thirteenth centuries a system of central administration was established in England which led to the creation of the very fine medieval archives housed at Chancery Lane, which over a century of publishing and scholarly interpretation have made widely available. Although the crown in this period imposed its will on the localities through (for the most part) the sheriff of each county, there is no corresponding archive of medieval local public records, and what have survived in county record offices from the middle ages are essentially private muniments, of families, religious houses or chartered boroughs. They are much less voluminous and much less systematic in character than the medieval public records.

The Tudor revolution in government, from the 1530s onwards, greatly extended the scope of central administration in England, brought Wales within its ambit for the first time, and led to a vast increase in both the creation and preservation of records. At the same time the first steps were taken to create a system of local government, with parliament laying certain duties on the justices of each county (or larger borough) and the voluntary officials of each parish (or township). It is thus in this period, at least in well documented counties, that the official holdings of county record offices begin, supplementing what is available in private collections with quarter sessions and parish records. Up to 1660, however, central government and the higher courts of law continued to take a close interest in the localities, which is why for this period there remains much of local interest in the Public Record Office. After 1660, and more especially after the revolution of 1688, central government's interference in the affairs of local communities receded and did not reassert itself until well into the nineteenth century. It is for this reason that the eighteenth-century public records, mainly housed at Kew, seem much less useful for the local historian than those of the century before or the century after. It is in this period that the administration of local communities lay largely in their own hands, either through the parish or the county, and for which the most important sources for local history are often private collections of family and estate records or business papers. Even in the early period of the Industrial Revolution (say 1760–1830) central government sources for local history remain limited.

All this was to change later in the nineteenth century as a result of a transformation of government and administration, at both national and local level, more revolutionary than that of the sixteenth century. From the 1830s to the first world war central government was vastly extended and took a closer interest in local communities —through for example the new administrative departments dealing with poor law, public health or education—than it had since before 1660. Thus central government archives once again become useful for local history. At the same time the system of local administration through the county and parish, established by the Tudors and modified by their successors, was completely overhauled as new institutions were established and existing ones revitalised, creating the local administrative records described in Chapter 3. Private muniments, especially those of landed families, also become much bulkier in the nineteenth century, which is why local record offices have a far larger quantity of both deposited and official records for this period than for any earlier century. Since 1914, and especially since 1945, there has in effect been a continuing revolution in government, creative archives on a scale which overshadows even that of the later nineteenth century.

The implications for the local historian of this pattern of record creation, at national and local level in England since the eleventh century, and in Wales since the sixteenth, may be summarised thus. From Domesday Book to the Dissolution (1086–1540) local material is limited in England to private muniments and for most Welsh communities hardly exists; the records of central government contain much relating to localities which is available in print in one form or another. From the mid-sixteenth century to the mid-nineteenth there is a growing bulk of material in local custody; for the first half of this period the enlarged public records contain a wealth of material relating to local communities, whereas after 1700 they become less useful. Finally, from about 1830 to 1914 (and beyond) there is a wealth of material, private and official, in local record offices, and a great deal in the Public Record Office. An overview of this kind may seem irrelevant to the beginner who simply wishes to trace the history of his house or find out when his great-grandfather was born, but if his interest develops he should appreciate how the pattern of record creation has changed over the centuries, why some periods are better documented than others, and why for some centuries one relies more heavily on the PRO and for others on a local repository.

Some other national institutions

The local historian visiting London for a few days may arrive either with specific references to material he is interested in in places as well as, or other than, the PRO, or at least in the hope of checking other repositories for relevant items. Thus it may be helpful to say something about a few of the many other libraries and record offices in the capital and about some national repositories outside London.

The institution which the beginner is perhaps most likely to have come across in scouring the footnotes to secondary sources is the Department of Manuscripts of the British Library, formerly the British Museum and still often cited as 'BM'. Despite the change of name the collection remains where it has been for a very long time, on the ground floor of the British Museum in Great Russell Street. Admission to the Students' Room of the Manuscript Department is by ticket, for which one should make written application in advance. It is much easier to get a ticket for the Manuscript Department than for the Reference Division of the British Library (the old BM Library), which is virtually impossible for anyone who could use another library. If you are working on a topic which requires the resources of the Manuscript Department, or have references to particular documents in the collection, you will normally be given a ticket. In the latter case, of course, it may be simpler to write asking about the cost of photocopies.

The manuscript collections of the British Library are rather different in character from those of either the PRO or a local repository. Although there are a few administrative records in the BL, the bulk of the collections is essentially 'private', consisting of the personal or political papers of statesmen, soldiers, sailors and the like; literary and musical manuscripts; and historical and antiquarian collections. The last category, which is likely to be of most interest to local historians, has brought into the library large quantities of medieval documents, especially the cartularies (manuscript volumes into which title deeds were copied) of religious houses, which were salvaged by antiquaries after the Dissolution. As well as manuscripts, there is also a large collection of mostly medieval charters which includes deeds relating to every county in England. These have often been included in nineteenth-century published calendars relating to a particular county, although of course the collection has been added to since most such books were published, while modern practice is to publish more topographical detail from medieval deeds than was the case a century ago.

The system of references and finding-aids at the BL also differs from that in use at the PRO or a local record office. In the first place, almost all manuscripts either arrive as bound volumes or are made up into volumes at the library. Except in the case of charters, a reader is normally presented with a volume rather than a box of loose documents. Most of the deeds form a series called simply 'Additional Charters', plus a serial number, although there are some smaller sequences, such as the Egerton Charters, with their own numbering. A similar plan is followed with the manuscripts. Whereas in a local record office the papers of (say) Sir Robert Peel would have been given a separate deposit number, in the British Museum they were simply made up into volumes and given the next block of numbers in the vast collection of Additional Manuscripts. The term 'Additional' (as in Add.Ch. or Add.MSS. in footnotes) implies that some other material was there in the first place: these are the Harleian Manuscripts (and a smaller collection of Harleian Charters) assembled by Robert Harley, whose magnificent collection of medieval and later manuscripts forms one of the nucleii around which the rest of the collection has been built since 1753. The collections of Sir Robert Cotton are another. The Harleian Manuscripts are especially rich sources for heraldry and genealogy, and the first reference to BL holdings a local historian comes across will often be a copy of a herald's visitation for his county in this collection.

There is an impressive and reasonably straighforward set of catalogues to the BL collections, which is available in most university and larger public libraries. A catalogue of the Harleian MSS was published by the Record Commission in the early nineteenth century, followed by a similar publication by the Trustees of the British Museum for the first group of Additional MSS. The Museum issued further catalogues over the following century, a process continued by the British Library Board. These describe each volume of Additional or other manuscripts in turn and are indexed. If you are tracing the history of a parish, or looking for some fairly well known individual, and can find a complete set of BL catalogues in a local library, it does not take long to search all the indexes and then turn to the descriptions of the relevant volumes to follow up references. The same is true of the charter catalogues, certainly in searches for parishes. At the library itself there are consolidated card indexes for all the published catalogues.

A search for a particular place at the BL may well reveal a block of Additional MSS which form antiquarian collections for your county. Since there were no local record offices until the present century and no public libraries until the late nineteenth, the papers of earlier antiquaries have sometimes ended up in the British Library, even though their scope is entirely local. In a few cases local studies libraries have acquired this sort of material on microfilm, otherwise it is available only in London and may not be catalogued in as much detail as a local historian might like. The older collections for a county history (now in the British Library), whether the work was eventually published or not, are generally much more valuable than the more modern material of the same kind found in local libraries (p. 34). There may well be extensive genealogical notes for a large number of families, including drawings of coats of arms; an antiquary may have made careful ink and wash sketches of local churches before Victorian rebuilding, or views of field monuments now much altered. Unpublished collections assembled by the major historian of your county may be well known, but material belonging to lesser local antiquaries may hardly have been used. One collection of general interest is that containing the papers of Daniel and Samuel Lysons, the promoters of the abortive *Magna Britannia* project of the early nineteenth century, covering not only the counties for which volumes were published but also those alphabetically beyond Devonshire for which nothing appeared. They include both notes from records and correspondence with local clergy in search of information.

Another class of material for which the BL has long been well known are heralds' visitations, the books compiled by officers of the College of Arms during tours of the counties in the sixteenth century and the first half of the seventeenth: these contain not merely the arms and pedigrees of gentle families but often also notes on heraldic decoration in domestic and church buildings and on church monuments. Most of the official visitation records are at the College of Arms but because of their antiquarian interest the books were widely pirated and dozens of copies, usually inferior to those at the College, exist in the Harleian Manuscripts and elsewhere. In the late nineteenth century it was popular to publish visitations for particular counties, and this became the main activity of the Harleian Society, which is still in existence. Most nineteenth-century editions of visitations are inaccurate transcripts of poor copies, especially those published other than by the Harleian Society, and there have been few scholarly modern editions (perhaps a sign of changing antiquarian taste). In counties with a classic history the substance of visitation pedigrees will usually appear in the accounts of families whose arms were recorded, or there may be an edition, good or bad, of a visitation for your county published separately. If neither is the case, and you are interested in a family whose arms and pedigree were recorded by the heralds, it may be worth looking at visitation books in the British Library or elsewhere.

The most authoritative source of information on heraldic matters is, of course, still the College of Arms, which can be found in an attractive seventeenth-century building in the City (Queen Victoria Street). As well as the main collection of visitation books, the College also houses its own archives, the papers of many past officers of arms, a fine reference library, and a considerable quantity of more general antiquarian collections relating to many parts of the country. There is a brief published guide. Traditionally, the College of Arms, was reluctant to allow searchers to use its collections directly and one had to work, at some expense, through one of the officers. While it remains a private rather than public repository, most users would probably agree that there has been a distinct change in atmosphere at the college in the last ten years. Local historians who wish to pursue some enquiry there, preferably not directly heraldic or genealogical, will find the Registrar and Librarian (who is also a herald) helpful and co-operative. Members of the college naturally still charge for their services in tracing pedigrees or making applications for grants of arms to private clients, although it seems unlikely that they have benefited from the upsurge of interest in genealogy of the last few years to anything like the same extent as did their late Victorian predecessors during the last such revival.

Local historians particularly interested in antiquarian papers will probably also wish to explore two other national repositories. Both the Bodleian Library in Oxford, and Cambridge University Library, have substantial manuscript collections, the former being especially rich in topographical material, not merely for Berks, Bucks and Oxon but for the whole country. The published finding aids for the two university libraries are not widely available elsewhere but one can obviously follow up specific references by correspondence and, if there is something you wish to look at, ask for a reader's ticket or order photocopies. Local historians in the Thames Valley and East Anglia will soon appreciate the special position, which is beyond the scope of a general guide, of the Bodleian and of CUL in the pattern of local record holding (the latter, for example, is a diocesan record office).

Returning to London, a few other places likely to be visited by local historians may be mentioned briefly, although some, such as the headquarters of the Registrar General's department (St Catherine's House, Strand WC2) or its near neighbour at Somerset House (the Principal Registry of the Family Division, where wills since 1858 are to be found) have already been described (pp. 64–5) and are in any case very well known from genealogical manuals. Most investigators interested in railways and canals will by now have grasped that the British Transport Historical Records are no longer to be found over Royal Oak underground station but are in the PRO at Kew, with all the references changed (p. 71). Another source for transport history is the proceedings before committees of the House of Lords on canal and railway bills, through which most local historians first encounter the House of Lords Record Office in the Palace of Westminster. Most of the archives of the House of Commons were destroyed by fire in 1834, but those of the Lords include unpublished minutes recording the investigation by committees of the house into bills authorising the construction of canals and railways in the late eighteenth century and the nineteenth. Like the plans deposited with clerks of the peace for such schemes (p. 89), of which another copy also had to go to Parliament, these committees include many concerned with bills which were ultimately unsuccessful. For anyone seriously pursuing the history of transport in his area they are a useful source, since witnesses went into considerable detail about trade and the likely benefits from the project, and were sometimes local coal- or iron-masters who discussed the fortunes of their own business.

There is no published list of canal and railway committee minutes in the House of Lords and the best way to identify material is to follow a scheme through Parliament, from its first introduction as a bill to its abandonment or to royal assent. The intricacies of eighteenth- and nineteenth-century local bill procedure are too complicated to explain here but with a little practice can be grasped from the *Journals* of the two Houses of Parliament; these can be found in the larger reference libraries and will contain the substance of any petitions sent in for or against a bill, which are often extremely useful (if partisan) comments on the pattern of local trade. One then writes to the House of Lords Record Office to see what unpublished papers, if any, survive from the committee stage. Local bills were not normally debated on the floor of the house and so are not referred to in the published *Parliamentary Debates* (*Hansard*), which form the almost verbatim record of proceedings, whereas the *Journals* are in the nature of minute-books. The House of Lords is not the place to go merely to read the *Journals* or to explore the immense wealth of published nineteenth-century Parliamentary Papers (alias Sessional Papers, Blue Books, Royal Commissions, Select Committees, etc). This material needs a book of its own to provide even a brief explanation of its arrangement, content and value for local history, and several guides have been published. Complete sets of Parliamentary Papers exist in only a handful of national libraries, but some of the major city reference libraries have good collections and there have been various reprint and microform projects in recent years. Similarly, printed sets of Acts of Parliament are available in public libraries, while the relevant local and personal Acts or private Acts in which most local historians tend to be more interested (since it was these that authorised canal, railway, gas- and water-works schemes, or allowed for the sale of an entailed estate) can usually be found in county record offices, since the clerk of the peace generally had his own law library.

Local historians of nonconformity may well find the holdings of their local record office disappointing, partly owing to the poor survival of chapel records compared to those of the established church but also because some denominations collect material into a central repository. The main centre for Quaker archives, for example, is Friends' House, Euston Road. Professor Stephens's book provides probably the best guide to this rather complicated subject.

This brief catalogue by no means exhausts the range of national institutions where a local historian may find material relevant to his particular, and possibly highly specialised, enquiry. The best available guide to record offices, that published by Jeremy Gibson, lists 17 places in central London alone, apart from the many excellent public libraries in the capital, some of which have large manuscript holdings. These, however, like the collections of the Greater London Record Office (40 Northampton Road, EC1) or the City of London Records Office (Guildhall, EC1, but not identical with the Guildhall Library), will be of most interest either to local historians pursuing London topics or to fairly experienced researchers for whom this book is not intended. Beginners do not usually want to look at material in the more specialised London repositories, but they should know something about the PRO, the British Library Department of Manuscripts and a few other places.

Since this book is aimed at local historians in Wales as well as England, it would be wrong to conclude without mentioning the National Library of Wales at Aberystwyth, which for the principality fulfils some of the functions of the PRO, is partly analogous to the BL, and is to some extent a 'super county record office' for Wales. Unfortunately, despite the library's national status, most local historians in Wales can actually get to London more easily than Aberystwyth, especially by train. Because of this, the transfer of the records of the court of great sessions of Wales and certain other Welsh public records from the PRO to the National Library has not necessarily made for greater use of the material. The library is also the provincial and diocesan record office for the Church in Wales, which means that it houses the probate records and bishops' transcripts from all four historic Welsh dioceses, as well as other non-parochial material (p. 62). In Powys (formerly Brecon, Radnor and Montgomery), despite the establishment of a record office, the NLW remains the repository for parish registers, although quarter sessions records for the three constituent counties have been returned to local custody. The library also has the quarter sessions records of these three counties. Apart from its official annd diocesan records, the National Library's 'gifts, deposits and purchases' are comparable to those of a particularly well endowed English county office. Many of the larger Welsh family and estate collections are at the NLW rather than a local office, and the library has substantial quantities of literary, antiquarian, political and other manuscripts, including some

Welsh nonconformist archives. The holdings of its manuscript department are organised on lines similar to those of an English country office, with typescript (occasionally printed and published) lists to which there is a card index in the library. The publication of indexes to its probate holdings has only just begun. The National Library offers a friendly and helpful service to local historians who manage to get to Aberystwyth, and goes to a good deal of trouble in answering postal enquiries. Its photocopying facilities are comprehensive and cheaper than those of the PRO, but can sometimes be very slow.

Chapter Seven
WRITING AND PUBLICATION

This chapter concerns two topics to which beginners rarely give much thought and which most amateurs never do anything about. It is, unfortunately, only too easy to carry on collecting information, possibly for years, without taking any steps to write up your discoveries, whether you are simply working for your own amusement or are supposed to be preparing a higher degree dissertation. The part-time amateur enthusiast does not even have the inducement of a degree at the end of the day or the pressure of a supervisor to get on and write something, and may well take the view that he has nothing to say of interest to anyone except himself. If he is working on the history of his own family he may well be right in that belief but in most other cases any piece of work done with reasonable care and thoroughness will be of some interest to someone somewhere, if they know about it. Even an account of your house may make a short article for a local magazine. False modesty has some charm; a more irritating trait is the refusal to publish anything for fear of letting others know of your discoveries. It is a mark of the worst kind of antiquarianism to regard knowledge as a species of private property and to refuse to talk about and share your research with others. It is also usually counter-productive, since publication can often stimulate new discoveries and even a talk to a local organisation can encourage others to pass on information. Another excuse for never publishing anything is that you haven't finished. This is also bogus. Research is never finished—that is not how historical knowledge works—but all local historians get to a point where they have something to say, even if all the loose ends have not been tied up and you may wish to write a fuller account of the same topic five years later. The accumulations of antiquarian notes in most libraries referred to in Chapter 2 (p. 34) should be a sufficient warning against never writing anything, at least for those local historians who really do want to be more than aimless antiquaries.

The local historian who never writes anything may claim that he is waiting until he has completed the history of his parish before producing one large book on his life's work. This is again an unsound basis on which to proceed. Apart from the likelihood of dying or losing interest before you have finished the definitive history of anywhere, you will almost certainly find that the complete history of a parish is unpublishably long, mainly for financial reasons; it will probably be utterly unreadable too. It is very difficult to write a consistently interesting village history from Domesday Book to the Great War, for reasons that will have become clear in the chapters on source material. All local historians soon come across the sort of parish history (*fl.* 1870–1914) which begins with the complete (usually untranslated and unexplained) text of the relevant part of Domesday Book, followed after a couple of pages on the Black Death in England by a transcript of the first parish register, commencing in 1558. Apart from a manorial descent lifted from the county history, most chapters on the middle ages in a book like this contain little of substance and nothing of interest. It is a basic sign of weakness in any historical writing to let the material dominate the narrative, although this still happens in so many village histories. There will be virtually nothing on the medieval period, then a great wad of inaccurately transcribed probate inventories, wills and churchwardens' accounts, followed by another gap for the eighteenth century, perhaps punctuated by some quarter sessions material from a published calendar. Nine-tenths of the book will be devoted to the period after 1800, especially those years with magnetic attraction for the village antiquary: 1841, 1851, 1861 and 1871. The book usually concludes with the author's own recollections of the village forty years ago, the work of the Home Guard during the last war, and pictures of the Coronation of 1953 and Silver Jubilee of 1977, which were probably marked by planting either a tree or a new seat on the village green. If a history of this kind succeeds in getting into print, either because of the personal wealth of the author or the misguided generosity of the parish council, it will be bought eagerly by the 500 or so subscribers whose names will be printed at the back (where the unsuspecting might have looked for an index, which these books never have). The happy purchasers will hurry home with their autographed copy (25p extra for church funds), open the book at Chapter 1, find themselves baffled by the misspelt geological terms, misunderstood archaeological discoveries and out-of-date early medieval history subsumed under the heading 'From the earliest times to the Norman Conquest' and put the book away never to pick it up again. Local history will thus have lost another 500 sympathetic readers.

Books of this kind do still get published, especially in the wealthier parts of the country, despite all the advice given to amateur local historians about what to write and how to present their information. If you are interested in the general history of your parish—and there is nothing wrong with this in itself—rather than in some thematic topic, do not think in terms of producing a complete village history in one large, handsomely printed and bound volume. Even if you live long enough to finish it and have the money to publish it, the result is still likely to be very boring. There are many better ways of both writing and publishing local history.

The approach of the competent amateur towards publication is usually rather different from that of the professional, or would-be academic. The latter frequently tries to disguise articles on local topics, which after all do not take as much time or effort to write as those on general problems, with grandiose titles, especially when submitting them to the more prestigious journals. Thus 'New light on rural depopulation in the later middle ages' will actually be based on one set of manor court rolls, but with a title like that it has a fair chance of getting into *Past and Present*, if not the *Economic History Review*, whereas 'The manor of Barset, 1350–1500', which may be just as thorough an analysis of the same documents (it may even be the same article with the rejection slips removed) sounds from the start as if it is destined for the *Barsetshire Archaeological Journal*. This is an affectation not to be copied by the experienced amateur whose work may well be of comparable standard to that of many higher degree students. Local work is best published in local journals where local people will read it, whence it will be listed in national bibliographies read by scholars looking for case-studies to illuminate general questions.

The top tier of local publishing has for a very long time been occupied by the county journals, whose history is outlined in Chapter 1 (pp. 18–19). These are now generally edited to a high standard and mostly publish a combination of archaeological reports, for which substantial public subsidies can be collected, and historical articles, which usually have to be financed entirely by the publishing society. The journals normally appear annually and are distributed to the society's members, whose numbers will probably lie between 500 and 2,000, depending on the wealth of the county and the length of time the society has been established. County journals are also subscribed to by most university libraries and articles in them are guaranteed a good circulation in this country and abroad. A more recent development has been the publication of three 'regional' history journals, *Northern History*, *Southern History* and *Midland History*. By contrast with these newer periodicals, the county journals may seem old-fashioned, but they have been around for a long time and remain a good outlet for the able amateur local historian doing worthwhile work on his area.

The beginner reading this book is probably not thinking of sending articles to the county journal, nor of offering to edit a volume for the local record society, which in some counties shares the 'heavy' end of local history publishing with the archaeological society. Just because he does not see himself in these terms does not mean that there will be no suitable outlet for his work. Most county societies, or alternatively some other body such as a federation of village local history groups, publish a magazine which solicits, indeed is usually desperate for, contributions on a more modest scale than those sought by the editor of the county journal. These publications, which tend to go under names like the *Loamshire Historian* or *Barsetshire Miscellany*, may be duplicated from typescript or printed more ambitiously. The most important point about them is that they are designed as an outlet for the main run of amateur local history, not for substantial county journal length articles or the fourth best chapter of someone's thesis. They will not usually be interested in a complete history of your village, especially if it would have to be printed in 24 instalments, but would welcome a few thousand words, preferably with illustrations, on a local ironworks which you have been studying, or a short account of a village school which has just closed. The editor will also prefer the article to be submitted in typescript with some indication of sources used, but otherwise these magazines have few pretensions to scholarship. They are a vehicle for amateur work which will interest their two or three hundred readers, and they occasionally publish an article which attracts wider attention. They are the best place for a beginner who has completed some modest project to seek publication, not least because they do not normally involve the author in any financial risk or effort beyond submitting a typescript. Before looking at local history publications that involve both, it may be useful to say something about how to tackle a short article for a local journal.

Some of the most important advice about writing local history was given in the chapter on starting research (pp. 26–30). If you are going to make anything out of your work later it is vital to keep a note of sources, whether in a library or record office. It is also essential, certainly with a project that is going to last any length of time, to order your notes in a coherent manner, probably by subject, so that when you come to write up you can find all the material to do with a particular topic in one place, preferably in chronological order, from which you can then draft an article, pamphlet or whatever. As far as actual writing is concerned, it is impossible to say more in a book about local history than appears in any book on English composition. Most people, once they have been out of full-time education for any length of time, and unless they are journalists or have occasion to write continuous prose in the course of their job, find writing difficult. You can read books on English usage, on how to write essays, on how to write well, on how to write clearly. They should all help, but you will probably still find writing a short article very much harder than collecting the material for it. This is precisely why it is better to start in a modest way with a piece on one particular topic, or you are unlikely ever to start, unless forced to do so by, for example, the requirements of an extramural diploma course, for which an 8,000 word dissertation may be needed at the end of the second or third year. This is of course why the old-fashioned village antiquary never writes anything, or in the end simply cobbles together his notes and transcripts and calls that a parish history. One folder of notes on a single subject is very much easier to make something of than an accumulation of many years divided between several boxes.

When some more specific advice is often welcomed by beginners is in the citation of sources. As the chapters on libraries and record offices explained, there is nothing mysterious about how to cite either printed works or manuscripts. For books and articles you give the normal bibliographical details (author, title, etc) which you should have written at the head of your notes, plus a page reference, unless you are citing the work as a whole. It is for this purpose, as well as to enable the reader to check back to the source, that notes taken from published work should include the page number. For manuscripts you normally cite the call-number given the document by the record office in which it is kept, prefaced by the name of the repository. In an article where documents are repeatedly cited from the same office, it is usual to shorten the name of the office in second and subsequent references, or give a list of abbreviations at the start of the footnotes. In practice, most readers of *Barsetshire Miscellany* will know what 'BRO' means, although the editor of the *Bartsetshire Arch. Journal* will want '(hereafter BRO)' after the full name of the office in the first reference. While most documents in local record offices have alphanumeric reference numbers it is sometimes more help to the reader to say what the document actually is, so that he may judge how reliable a source it is. Thus, 'BRO, D801, PI2' may well be enough for an archivist to realise that a parish register is being cited, but for the average reader it is simpler to say that it is the parish register for such-and-such place in the footnote.

The beginner writing an article for a local magazine and using footnote references for the first time should avoid picking up certain bad habits found in much pseudo-academic local history. In the case of references to published work it is no longer a sign of scholarship to use *Op.cit.*, *Loc.cit.* and their friends (mentioned earlier, p. 29); they are mostly long overdue for retirement. The standard county history should be cited as J. Smith, *History of Barsetshire* (1791), III, p. 191, on its first appearance, then as Smith, *Barsetshire*, III, p. 200 the next time. The Rev. J. J. Smith's article on 'Bartsetshire monumental effigies of the later 15th century', *Barsetshire Arch. Journal*, XII (1886), 1–65, may be cited thus if you are mentioning it for the first time and want to refer to the whole article; if one particular tomb is referred to later on it can come down to 'Smith, "Monumental effigies", p. 32'. If you are citing several different articles from the county journal, *BAJ* will probably be intelligible to your local readers after an initial reference in full. If you have two *successive* references to the same work and the *first* note cites only one title, it is still convenient to use '*Ibid.*' ('the same') in the second; this becomes ambiguous if there is more than one reference in the first note, although '*Ibid*; cf. also . . .' is permissible in the second. *Ibid.* should not be used in a succession of manuscript references.

Another bad habit, known to all examiners of MA theses and most book reviewers, is the device of the 'transparent secondary source'. There is nothing necessarily wrong in relying on a statement in a published book, as long as you say honestly where the information is from, and in practice someone writing for *Barsetshire Miscellany* is unlikely to go to the PRO to check that the author of a parish history in VCH correctly interpreted the evidence of the 1670 hearth tax for your village. What is wrong is not to copy a statement of the number of taxpayers from VCH but to copy the PRO call-number from the footnote in VCH and put that in your reference. In many cases this will look obviously bogus, especially if you transcribe the reference incorrectly. If you have used a secondary source, cite the secondary source, not the primary source in the other author's own reference.

One final piece of advice about footnotes, given to all intending higher degree students and just as applicable to local historians: use references to tell the reader where you have got a piece of information from, not to continue the text of the article at the bottom of the page or at the end. Some footnotes will obviously have comment in them beyond a mere title or reference—'I am indebted to Mr J. Smith for help in reading this document'; 'This parish was in Loamshire until 1889 when the county boundary was moved'—but do not use a footnote to go off at a tangent.

The advice given here and in similar books about how to compose a neatly turned footnote may miss the point: that many beginners simply want to be told where to put the damn things in the first place. In articles intended for fairly modest magazines it is in fact often possible to avoid using them at all and much simpler, in work based on only a few sources, to rely on references worked into the text. 'According to Smith (*Barsetshire*, III, p. 191) . . .', or 'A rental of 1735 now in the Barsetshire Record Office (D967/E45) reveals that . . .' is likely to be perfectly acceptable in *Barsetshire Miscellany* and is just as clear as a statement in the text supported by a footnote containing the same information, which is what the *Barsetshire Arch. Journal* will prefer. This technique is halfway towards the method of citation used in scientific publication (including archaeology, although not always in local journals) known as the author-date system, in which the county history would be cited as 'Smith 1791' in the text and at the end of the article would appear in a list of sources as 'Smith, J. 1791. *History of Barsetshire*'. If you are using conventional footnotes, try to keep the reference numbers to a minimum, especially in a duplicated magazine which will not have the facility for setting proper index numbers but will put them in brackets in the text. If possible, keep them to the end of sentences, where they least disrupt the text. Thus the statement that 'John Smith was tenant of Townend Farm in 1735, 1741 and 1750, but had left by 1760' can be supported by one reference to four rentals or leases; there is no need to put an index number after each date. Any precise statement such as this should have a reference; what is not necessary is to support general observations. Readers of 'The Barsetshire Yeomanry in France, 1914–16' will take your word for it that the first world war broke out in August 1914 but will appreciate a reference to a newspaper article describing the Barsetshires' departure for the front, on which you have relied heavily for local detail.

With this simple advice, any local historian should be able to compose and annotate a short article on a limited topic for a magazine published by one of the societies in his area. If he is in doubt as to the standard expected, there will be copies of the magazine in the local library which will indicate the sort of contributions included. Even if you have only put together notes on the history of your house, or the development of your suburb as revealed in a sequence of maps, it is worth writing up your finding to bring the work to a conclusion and to pass on information to others.

The editor to whom you submit a piece such as this may well ask for illustrations, since most local history magazines are now printed by a method that allows the reproduction of at least maps and line drawings and possibly also half-tone photographs. The county journals are progressively converting to production methods that accommodate half-tones and text on the same page, whereas in the past editors kept plates to the minimum because of the extra expense. It is not usually very difficult to find some illustrations for almost any local article: either go out and take a couple of clear black and white photographs yourself, or have an old photograph in the library copied, or an engraving or some other picture. What most people find much harder, and frequently duck out of doing to the detriment of the piece of work as a whole, is to provide a map. Most articles in local history magazines, indeed most published local history, would benefit from the inclusion of more maps. Sometimes it is possible to reproduce an old map directly: tithe maps and the earlier editions of the Ordnance Survey can be copied without technical or legal difficulties. More often, however, what is needed is a simple line-drawn sketch map, usually based on the Ordnance Survey, which marks the features specifically mentioned in the article rather than the landscape as a whole. It is beyond the scope of this book to give detailed advice on how to draw such maps but there are clear guides available on how to produce acceptable results with simple equipment and no particular artistic skill. Like writing footnotes, there is nothing complicated about producing maps for local history and they greatly improve almost any piece of work. They do not normally add to the cost of publication, since a page of line drawing and a page of text are usually charged for at the same rate by printers.

The beginner whose first venture into local history publishing is to send a six-page article to *Barsetshire Miscellany* on his village school will probably not be greatly concerned about, or knowledgeable of, the cost of getting magazines such as this into print. He will certainly not be concerned with the economics of publishing a parish history of 156 pages or a 96 page book of old photographs. The economics of journal publishing are, however, an obsessive concern of all committees of the larger societies, whose editors and treasurers struggle on from year to year looking for cheaper printers, another source of grant-aid, or occasionally more members. A 36 page stapled magazine reproduced from typescript is not usually confronted with similar problems. As the local historian becomes more ambitious, however, or as he becomes involved in a local group which either publishes a magazine of its own or is seeking to publish something, he will find himself involved in discussions about printing, publishing and finance.

Despite the unprecedented popular interest in the subject, it remains true, as it always has been, that few mainstream publishers are interested in local history. This is partly because most amateur village histories are so unreadable and partly because their appeal is really so limited. Even with modern printing techniques, which make short-run bookwork more economic than it used to be, a village history of 150 pages selling perhaps 700 copies out of a print of 1000 is not going to interest a reputable publisher. The small number of firms that do claim to be interested in getting amateur parish histories into print usually offer to do so on terms more advantageous to the publisher than the author, or invite the prospective reader to part with money some months before he receives a book. If you have £2500 to sink into your life's work on the history of your village and are not too worried as to whether you get the money back or not, you may as well deal directly with a printer and not put money into the hands of a little known publisher.

Similar advice applies to local groups seeking to publish a town or village history. It is almost always far better to raise the money yourselves, find a competent local printer, get the book published and sell it yourselves. Most of the sales will be to local people and with group effort it is usually possible to get rid of enough copies to break even. This may seem optimistic advice for a newly formed group, attracted but at the same time daunted by the prospect of writing a collaborative history of their town or village, but experience from many parts of the country suggests this is the best way of proceeding. So much work of this kind is now being published that a new group should be able to look at what has been produced recently in its own area and choose a printer, preferably one fairly close at hand, who will turn out an attractive piece of work. For a full-length book conventionally printed it is not usually worth producing less than 1000 copies and rarely feasible to consider more than 2000. Hardback binding with a dustjacket does not add greatly to the cost and does add to both the durability and saleability of the book. Reproducing the text from typescript rather than properly set type may save money, although not as much as is sometimes supposed, but it will certainly put off some potential customers. Illustrations are vital, and the preparation of decent maps time-consuming but essential for a book intended to be of more than antiquarian interest.

Actually getting the book through the press is the printer's job; having the funds to pay the printer and then being able to sell enough copies to recover your outlay are tasks which fall to the local group which decides to act as its own publisher. Raising money seems to frighten such groups more than is necessary. It is possible that a grant may be forthcoming from a local authority, although I see no obvious reason why it should. (It is certain, incidentally, that no money will be forthcoming from a university extramural department. Their contribution to local history is through teaching and advice, not giving grants for publication, and any publishing undertaken by a department is normally confined to work which its own tutors and students have done.) The whole range of fund-raising activities favoured by voluntary organisations (jumble sales, coffee mornings, wine and cheese parties, etc) can be called into play. One can try selling the book in advance on subscription although this rarely succeeds in raising all the money needed. Another method, which seems not to be used as much as it might be, is simply for the members of the group themselves to pool their own resources and guarantee the printer's bill collectively. For a small publication being produced in a prosperous southern English town by a group of whom most are employed or retired professional people, it should frankly not be very difficult to raise at least £1000 and possibly twice that from a group of guarantors. This is much simpler than organising fund-raising events and less demeaning than holding out the begging bowl down at the council offices.

Selling the book once it has appeared should not be too great a struggle if it is reasonably well written and attractively illustrated and printed. Much depends on the community in which you are working. In a small country town with a traditional stock-holding bookshop run by a reasonably interested resident proprietor it may be possible for him to act as the main outlet in return for the usual trade terms (one-third discount). If the only 'bookshops' in the neighbourhood are branches of multiple stationers forget it and sell the books yourself. It is always worth making an occasion of the actual publication of the book. Hold a public meeting, preferably with a lecture by the author and an exhibition of some kind. Have a large quantity of books on sale at the back of the hall and station the author there to autograph them. Try to get a photograph in the local paper. A well organised evening like this can often shift 25 or 30 per cent of the quantity you have to sell to break even and should stimulate interest resulting in sales in the following weeks.

Your customers, especially libraries and trade agents, have to know where to buy the book. For this reason it is important to print, usually on the back of the title-page, not only the name of the printer and the date of publication, but also the name of the publisher and the address from which copies can be ordered. A related point is that as soon as it is published, five copies of the book should be sent to the agent for the national libraries entitled to receive a copy of every book published in Britain, and one to the British Library Reference Division (see p. 161 for addresses). This may seem extravagant at the time but it is the law, and the BL copy will soon repay the investment by generating orders from libraries and booksellers who have seen the details listed in *British National Bibliography*, a comprehensive list compiled from accessions at the BL. It is usually worth sending a review copy to the local newspaper and possibly to the county local history magazine. *The Local Historian* has a section listing new publications, as does the more recently established *Local History*, a magazine published privately by a firm in Nottingham.

The suggestions made so far in this chapter, aimed mainly at groups who have produced a fairly substantial town or village history, possibly with different people writing different chapters, apply also to those who are merely aiming to publish a booklet, or series of booklets, on aspects of the history of their community. This is in fact often the best way of proceeding. Writing the *History of Barchester* in 256 handsome pages takes a long time; getting it published may involve a great deal of effort and money. Enthusiasm wanes over the years, people leave the area, dissension disrupts the group. Nothing gets published in the end. The same may apply to a group which sets up a local journal as a vehicle for members' research. The first issue of the *Barchester Historian* may be a great success but if the typist who prepared camera-copy in her lunch hour on the firm's IBM composer leaves to have a baby, of if the editor and business manager both move jobs to another part of the country, the second issue may be a year late. The third may have very few contributions because interest has slackened, and there may never be a fourth. On the other hand, if the Barchester Local History Study Group succeeds in publishing a 48 page, well printed, card-covered booklet on *Barchester in 1851* after a couple of years' work, and sells 500 copies at £2.50 a time, it has (a) achieved something tangible, (b) brought a piece of work to a satisfactory conclusion, (c) made some money for the future, and (d) not committed itself to more expenditure on a regular publication. There may then be sufficient enthusiasm to carry on with work for Barchester Papers No 2, on

Roman Barchester, and another fairly modest publication can be organised.

Working in this way is often the best plan for a new group, especially in a community on whose history little has been written in modern times. Members can see something in print fairly quickly as the result of their efforts, without having to raise large sums, and each of the active researchers can get on with his own pet project without interference from others. If someone finishes a good, self-contained essay on *Barchester Inns* it can be published as it stands, rather than put on one side for years as a chapter in a town history or rejected for the *Barchester Historian* because it would fill the entire magazine. If enthusiasm temporarily flags, or funds run low for a couple of years, a series such as this can be suspended without difficulty, whereas subscribers to a magazine become restive if they do not receive something each year for their money. There have been many highly successful local groups over the last twenty years publishing in this way, free from the constraints of filling an annual periodical which rapidly becomes a chore for the editor and a nightmare for the treasurer. Their research papers, occasional papers or whatever have together made a far greater contribution to the history of local communities than most of the monographs claiming to trace the history of a town from the earliest times to 1914, within the covers of one, usually very tedious, hardback book.

Below the level of a fairly substantial booklet there is a whole undergrowth of local history publishing undertaken by societies or individuals. Probably the most popular format is the ubiquitous 'trail', a folded single sheet or small pamphlet providing an itinerary around a town or village. Hundreds of these have been published and sold, although few people can claim actually to have seen someone following one of their trails round the town. The attraction of this sort of publication for a newly established group is that it requires virtually no outlay to produce and will usually be sold by any reasonably sympathetic retailer, who will be prepared to admit that people do occasionally come into his shop prepared to go up to 25p on a publication of local interest. Again, it serves to enhance members' interest, and that of others, in a local history group that has not been going long enough to think of publishing anything more ambitious. It is particularly important that a trail, or anything similar, be well printed and attractively illustrated, so that it catches attention on a bookstall. As with most other local history publishing, there is now so much material of this kind being produced that the prospective publisher should be able find several examples available locally as a guide to what constitutes a saleable piece of work.

The view of the local book trade, or its nearest equivalent, on marketing is often worth consulting before any publication is undertaken. Both commercial booksellers and those in charge of sales at museums and heritage centres have a well-honed rule of thumb as to what will sell in their shop. This will be based partly on appearance (people like 'proper books', not those with the text reproduced from typescript), partly on format (people do not like A4 pamphlets because they don't fit on bookshelves), but mainly on price. You will be told, *ex cathedra*, that people (often 'people round here' or, worse still, 'ordinary people', local historians being some how extraordinary) will spend £1 on a stapled card-covered booklet with a nice picture on the front, will perhaps spend £1.50 if the booklet has the name of their village in the title, but will not go beyond £2 under any circumstances. Local history groups have often proved these predictions wrong by publishing hugely successful hardback books at £10 a time, and certainly books of old photographs usually break out of this mould, but for the newly established group deciding how best to publish their first research paper, the advice is generally worth heeding.

This guide to self-publishing in local history may seem irrelevant to the needs of the individual amateur beginning research, but it has been included because many local historians soon find themselves involved in group projects and seek advice on publication. Working within a group is probably better than becoming a one-man publisher in any case. If the group is an extramural class the department may undertake the publication of a research project, otherwise it is for the group themselves to work out the best way of proceeding, taking into account local circumstances, how much money is available, and what members want to do. Self-publishing by a local group, whether through a pamphlet series or a magazine, is how most local historians first see their work in print, and the advice in this chapter may help both with the mechanics of writing local history in a simple but reasonably scholarly way, and in getting it published in an equally simple but nonetheless permanent and attractive form.

USEFUL ADDRESSES

This is not the place to list addresses of local record offices, much less the whereabouts of the shifting mass of amateur groups which form the backbone of voluntary local history throughout the country. Any reference library will have the names and addresses of local societies in your area, as well as details of museums, record offices and archaeological units. What may be useful here is to supply details of some of the national bodies in the field and a few other addresses local historians often ask for.

The only national organisation devoted solely to the promotion of local history is the British Association for Local History, Shopwyke Hall, Chichester, W. Sussex, which was established in 1982 as the successor to the now defunct Standing Conference for Local History. BALH has taken over publication of *The Local Historian*, details of which can be obtained from Shopwyke Hall, and sales of the SCLH's pamphlet series; in the Further Reading section below (pp. 163–9) I have given BALH as the publisher of these titles, although all were originally issued by the Standing Conference. An older voluntary body concerned with all aspects of the study of history in the Historical Association, 59a Kennington Park Road, London SE11, which publishes *History*, *Teaching History* and an extensive series of pamphlets, many of which are of great value to local historians. There are numerous national organisations concerned with more specialised aspects of the subject, whose addresses can be found most easily in the current issue of their journal. It may, however, be worth mentioning the British Records Association (18 Padbury Court, London E2 7EH), since several of their publications appear in the list of further reading, and two which have a substantial amateur membership: the Federation of Family History Societies (Federation of Family History Societies: 31 Seven Star Road, Solihull, W. Midlands) and the Association for Industrial Archaeology (Ironbridge Gorge Museum, Telford, Salop). The FFHS is an association of local genealogical societies but individuals may subscribe to its very useful twice-annual *Family History News and Digest*; the AIA has individual membership and can put people in touch with local industrial archaeology groups.

The national institutions whose collections are mentioned in Chapter 6 may be found at the following addresses:

Public Record Office, Chancery Lane, London WC2A 1LR, *and* Ruskin Avenue, Kew, Richmond, Surrey TW9 4DU.

British Library, Department of Manuscripts, Great Russell Street, London WC1B 3DG.

College of Arms, Queen Victoria Street, London EC4; address general enquiries to the Librarian (historical) or the Officer in Waiting (heraldic or genealogical).

Department of Western Manuscripts, Bodleian Library, Oxford OX1 3BG.

Department of Manuscripts, Cambridge University Library, West Road, Cambridge CB3 9DR.

House of Lords Record Office, London SW1A 0PW.

Department of Manuscripts and Records, National Library of Wales, Aberystwyth SY23 3BU.

For individuals or groups involved in self-publishing of local history there are two important addresses to remember: the International Standard Book Numbering Agency (C/o Whitakers, 12 Dyott Street, London WC1), who should be contacted before publication to obtain an ISBN for each title produced; and the agent who collects one copy of every book published on behalf of five of the six copyright libraries (see above, p. 157): A. T. Smail, 100 Euston Street, London NW1. The British Library collects copyright copies directly; in this case send a copy to the Copyright Receipt Office, British Library Reference Division, Great Russell Street, WC1.

The first two titles listed under the heading 'At the Record Office' in the Further Reading section (p. 164) are useful directories of national and local record repositories.

FURTHER READING

The following suggestions for further reading are arranged in broadly the same way as the text, with general works followed by those on more specialised topics. There is now a number of books on local history as a whole and a large literature of pamphlets and articles on particular topics. I have tried to confine this list to material which should be available in any public library with a local studies section, and references given in these books should provide leads to articles in a variety of scholarly journals or to major reference works for which the resources of a city or university library will be needed. I have not included articles in *The Local Historian* (pp. 22–3), although it is always worth scanning recent issues for material of general interest and most public libraries subscribe to the magazine. For further reading on topics for which nothing is listed here the two best books are usually either W. B. Stephens, *Sources for English Local History* (3rd edition, Cambridge, 1981), or *Group Projects in Local History*, edited by Alan Rogers (Folkestone, Dawson, 1977). Stephens is a better guide to printed and archival sources; *Group Projects* is stronger on fieldwork and topography and most of its ideas are applicable to individual as well as group work. The Historical Association has recently (1982) issued a fully revised 5th edition of its invaluable *Local History Handlist*, compiled by A. T. Hall, which is the only separately published large-scale bibliography for the subject.

Chapter 1. Local History Today

This chapter has two main themes: the present position of local history and its evolution since the sixteenth century. On the modern development of the subject the following works (listed in order of publication) may be of interest:

COX, J. C, *How to Write the History of a Parish*, London, Bemrose, 1879.

PUGH, R. B., *How to Write a Parish History*, Allen & Unwin, 1954.

HOSKINS, W. G., *Local History in England*, Longman, 1959; 2nd edition, 1972.

WEST, J., *Village Records*, 1962; 2nd edition, Chichester, Phillimore, 1982.

HOSKINS, W. G., *Provincial England*, Macmillan, 1963.

HOSKINS, W. G., *English Local History. The Past and the Future*, Leicester University Press, 1966.

EMMISON, F. G., *Archives and Local History*, Methuen, 1966.

FINBERG, H. P. R., and SKIPP, V. H. T., *Local History. Objective and Pursuit*, Newton Abbot, David & Charles, 1967.

DOUCH, R., *Local History and the Teacher*, Routledge, 1967.

IREDALE, D., *Local History Research and Writing. A Manual for Local History Writers*, Leeds, Elmfield Press, 1974.

RICHARDSON, J., *The Local Historian's Encyclopaedia*, New Barnet, Historical Publications, 1974.

ROGERS, A., *Approaches to Local History*, Longman, 1977.

STEPHENS, W. B., *Teaching Local History*, Manchester University Press, 1977.

ROGERS, A. (ed.) *Group Projects in Local History*, Folkestone, Dawson, 1977.

MACFARLANE, A., with HARRISON, S., and JARDINE, C., *Reconstructing Historical Communities*, Cambridge University Press, 1977.

STEPHENS, W. B., *Sources for English Local History*, 3rd edition, Cambridge University Press, 1981.

On antiquarianism since the sixteenth century there is a small but growing literature, which in addition to a number of articles includes the following:

DOUGLAS, D. C., *English Scholars*, Jonathan Cape, 1951.

FOX, L. (ed.), *English Historical Scholarship in the Sixteenth and Seventeenth Centuries*, Dugdale Society, 1956.

FUSSNER, F. S., *The Historical Revolution. English Historical Writing and Thought, 1580–1640*, Routledge, 1962.

MOIR, E. A. L., *The Discovery of Britain. The English Tourists, 1540–1840*, Routledge, 1964.

PUGH, R. B. (ed.), *Victoria History of the Counties of England. General Introduction*, Oxford University Press, 1970.

SIMMONS, J. (ed.), *English County Historians*, Wakefield, EP, 1978.

DANIEL, G. E, *A Hundred Years of Archaeology*, Duckworth, 1950.

KENDRICK, T. D., *British Antiquity*, Methuen, 2nd edition, 1970.

Chapter 2. At the Library

Most local studies libraries issue brief guides to their collections as a whole and to particular types of material. Larger libraries should also have the main general reference books on some of the sources described in this chapter:

HOBBS, J. L., *Local History and the Library*, Deutsch, 1962.

NORTON, J. E., *Guide to National and Provincial Directories of England*

and Wales, excluding London, published before 1856, Royal Historical Society, 1950.

GOSS, C. W. F., *The London Directories, 1677–1855,* London, Dennis Archer, 1932.

BRITISH LIBRARY, *Catalogue of the Newspaper Library,* 1975.

THE TIMES, *Tercentary Handlist of English and Welsh Newspapers, Magazines and Reviews, 1620–1919,* 1920.

MULLINS, E. L. C. (ed.), *A Guide to the Historical and Archaeological Publications of Societies in England and Wales, 1901–33,* Royal Historical Society, 1958.

MULLINS, E. L. C. (ED.), *Texts and Calendars: An Analytical Guide to Serial Publications,* Royal Historical Society, 1968.

BARLEY, M. W., *A Guide to British Topographical Collections,* Council for British Archaeology, 1974.

HMSO, *British National Archives,* issued periodically.

HMSO, *Publications at the Royal Commission on Historical Manuscripts,* issued periodically.

There is a large literature on the nineteenth-century censuses and the enumerators' books which are their best-known by-product:

GIBSON, J. S. W. (comp.), *Census Returns 1841, 1851, 1861, 1871, 1881. A Directory to Local Holdings,* Federation of Family History Societies, 1982.

GIBSON, J. S. W. and CHAPMAN, C., *Census Indexes and Indexing,* Federation of Family History Societies, 1981.

OFFICE OF POPULATION CENSUSES AND SURVEYS, *Guide to Census Reports: 1801–1966,* HMSO, 1977.

WRIGLEY, E. A. (ED.), *Nineteenth-century Society. Essays in the Use of Quantitative Methods for the Study of Social Data,* Cambridge University Press, 1972.

LAWTON, R. (ed.), *The Census and Social Structure. An Interpretive Guide to the Nineteenth-Century Censuses for England and Wales,* Cass, 1978.

Chapter 3. At the Record Office

This chapter touches on a variety of topics, many of which are well covered by publications issued by local offices describing their own holdings. On record offices themselves and general problems of using archives, such as palaeography, chronology and Latin, the following may be helpful:

GIBSON, J. S. W. and PESKETT, P., *Record Offices: How to Find Them,* Federation of Family History Societies, 1981.

HISTORICAL MANUSCRIPTS COMMISSION, *Record Repositories in Great Britain,* issued periodically.

EMMISON, F. G., *How to Read Local Archives, 1550–1700,* Historical Association, 1967.

HECTOR, L. C., *The Handwriting of English Documents*, new edition, Dorking, Kohler & Coombes, 1980.

NEWTON, K. C., *Medieval Local Records. A Reading Aid*, Historical Association, 1971.

MARTIN, C. T., *The Record Interpreter*, new edition, Dorking, Kohler & Coombes, 1976.

CHENEY, C. R. (ED.)., *Handbook of Dates for Students of English History*, Royal Historical Society, 1970.

POWICKE, F. M., and FRYDE, E. B., *Handbook of British Chronology*, Royal Historical Society, 1961.

GOODER, E. A., *Latin for Local History. An Introduction*, Longman, 1978.

LATHAM, R. E. (ed.), *Revised Medieval Latin Word List*, Oxford University Press, 1965.

Several books and pamphlets provide guides to the records of local administration, the Church, landownership and some of the other subjects mentioned in this chapter.

MUNBY, L. M. (ed.), *Short Guides to Records*, Historical Association, 1972.

TATE, W. E., *The Parish Chest*, Cambridge University Press, 1960.

KEITH-LUCAS, B., *English Local Government in the Nineteenth and Twentieth Centuries*, Historical Association, 1977.

EMMISON, F. G., and GRAY, I., *County Records*, Historical Association, 1961.

GIBSON, J. S. W. (comp.), *Quarter Sessions Records for Family Historians: A Select List*, Federation of Family History Societies, 1982.

OWEN, D. M., *The Records of the Established Church in England, excluding Parochial Records*, British Records Association, 1970.

HARVEY, J. H., *Sources for the History of a House*, British Records Association, 1974.

DIBBEN, A. A., *Title Deeds 13th-19th Centuries*, Historical Association, 1971.

STEEL, D. J. (ed.), *National Index of Parish Registers*, Society of Genealogists, 1968 onwards.

GIBSON, J. S. W., *Bishops' Transcripts and Marriage Licences, Bonds and Allegations. A Guide to their Location and Indexes*, Federation of Family History Societies, 1981.

WALCOT, M., and GIBSON, J. S. W., *Marriage Indexes. How to Find Them, How to Use Them, How to Compile One*, Federation of Family History Societies, 1980.

CAMP, A. J., *Wills and their Whereabouts*, Society of Genealogists, 1974.

GIBSON, J. S. W., *Wills and Where to Find Them*, Chichester, Phillimore, 1974.

GIBSON, J. S. W. *A Simplified Guide to Probate Jurisdiction: Where to*

Look For Wills, Federation of Family History Societies, 1980.

CAMP, A. J. (ed.), *An Index to the Wills Proved in the Prerogative Court of Canterbury, 1750–1800*, Society of Genealogists, 1976 onwards.

MILWARD, R., *A Glossary of Household, Farming and Trade Terms from Probate Inventories*, Derbyshire Record Society, 1982.

BURKE'S PEERAGE, *Burke's Family Index*, 1976.

WRIGLEY, E. A. (ed.), *An Introduction to English Historical Demography from the Sixteenth to Nineteenth Century*, Weidenfeld & Nicolson, 1966.

BARKER, T. C. and others, *Business History*, Historical Association, 1960.

Chapter 4. Maps

In addition to many local map bibliographies, published or kept on cards in a library or record office, there are several very useful general references in this field:

HARLEY, J. B., *Maps for the Local Historian. A Guide to British Sources*, British Association for Local History, 1972.

HARLEY, J. B., and PHILLIPS, C. W., *The Historian's Guide to Ordnance Survey Maps*, British Association for Local History, 1965.

CLOSE, C., *The Early Years of the Ordnance Survey*, new edition with introduction by J. B. Harley, Newton Abbot, David & Charles, 1969.

EVANS, E. J., *Tithes and the Tithe Commutation Act 1836*, British Association for Local History, 1978.

ROGER, E. M., *The Large Scale Maps of the British Isles, 1596–1850. A Union List*, Oxford, Bodleian Library, 1972.

BRITISH MUSEUM, *Catalogue of Printed Maps, Charts and Plans to 1964, 1967*.

Maps and Plans in the Public Record Office. I. British Isles c. 1410–1860, HMSO, 1967.

With maps may conveniently be coupled place-names:

EKWALL, E., *Concise Oxford Dictionary of English Place Names*, 4th edition, 1960.

SMITH, A. H., *English Place Name Elements*, English Place Name Society, 1956.

CAMERON, K., *English Place Names*, Batsford, 1977.

REANEY, P. H., *The Origin of English Place Names*, Routledge, 1960.

FIELD, J. *English Field-Names. A Dictionary*, Newton Abbot, David & Charles, 1972.

ADAMS, I. H., *Agrarian Landscape Terms. A Glossary for Historical Geography*, Institute of British Geographers, 1976.

ORDNANCE SURVEY, *Place Names on Maps of Scotland and Wales. A Glossary of the most common Gaelic and Scandinavian Elements used on*

Maps of Scotland and of the most common Welsh Elements used on Maps of Wales, 1973.

Chapter 5. Landscapes and Buildings

There is a very large literature on the field covered by this chapter. Some of the more general books on fieldwork in local history, landscape history and the relationship of history and archaeology include:

HOSKINS, W. G., *The Making of the English Landscape*, Hodder & Stoughton, 1955.

BERESFORD, M. W., *History on the Ground*, 2nd edition, Methuen, 1971.

BERESFORD, M. W., and ST JOSEPH, J. K., *Medieval England. An Aerial Survey*, Cambridge University Press, 1958.

HOSKINS, W. G., *Fieldwork in Local History*, Faber, 1967.

DYMOND, D. P., *Archaeology for the Historian*, Historical Association, 1967.

ROGERS, A., and ROWLEY, T. (ed.), *Landscapes and Documents*, British Association for Local History, 1974.

DYMOND, D. P., *Archaeology and History. A Plea for Reconciliation*, Thames & Hudson, 1974.

TAYLOR, C. C., *Fieldwork in Medieval Archaeology*, Batsford, 1974.

PLATT, C., *Medieval Archaeology in England. A Guide to the Historical Sources*, Isle of Wight, Pinhorns, 1969.

Recent work on the medieval landscape or aspects thereof:

BERESFORD, M. W., and HURST, J. G. (ed.), *Deserted Medieval Villages. Studies*, Lutterworth Press, 1971.

HOOPER, M. D., and others, *Hedges and Local History*, British Association for Local History, 1971.

BAKER, A. R. H., and BUTLIN, R. A. (ed.), *Studies of Field Systems in the British Isles*, Cambridge University Press, 1973.

RUSSELL, R. C., *The Logic of Open Field Systems*, British Association for Local History, 1975.

TAYLOR, C. C., *Fields in the English Landscape*, Dent, 1975.

SAWYER, P. H. (ed.), *Medieval Settlement. Continuity and change*, Edward Arnold, 1976.

The following titles represent some of the work on industrial archaeology likely to be of permanent interest, either as practical handbooks or as intelligent discussions of the subject:

RIX, M. M., *Industrial Archaeology*, Historical Association, 1967.

BUCHANAN, R. A., *Industrial Archaeology in Britain*, Harmondsworth, Penguin, 1972.

COSSONS, N., *The BP Book of Industrial Archaeology*, Newton Abbott, David & Charles, 1975.

MAJOR, J. K., *Fieldwork in Industrial Archaeology*, Batsford, 1975.

PANNELL, J. P. M., *The Techniques of Industrial Archaeology*, 2nd edition, revised by J. K. MAJOR, Newton Abbot, David & Charles, 1974.

TRINDER, B. S., *The Making of the Industrial Landscape*, Dent, 1982.

On vernacular architecture see the following:

BARLEY, M. W., *The English Farm House and Cottage*, Routledge, 1961.

WOOD, M. E., *The English Medieval House*, Phoenix House, 1965.

EDEN, P. M. G., *Small Houses in England, 1520–1820. Towards a Classification*, Historical Association, 1969.

BRUNSKILL, R. W., *Illustrated Handbook of Vernacular Architecture*, Faber, 1970.

PARKER, V., *The English House in the Nineteenth Century*, Historical Association, 1970.

HARVEY, N., *A History of Farm Buildings in England and Wales*, Newton Abbott, David & Charles, 1970.

CHAPMAN, S. D. (ed.), *The History of Working Class Housing*, Newton Abbot, David & Charles, 1971.

SMITH, J. T., and YATES, E. M., *On the Dating of English Houses from External Evidence*, reprinted from *Field Studies*, Vol.2, No.5, 1968, by E. W. Classey, 353 Hanworth Road, Hampton, Middlesex, 1972.

CLIFTON-TAYLOR, A., *The Pattern of English Building*, Faber, 1972.

ADDYMAN, P., and MORRIS, M. K. (ed.), *The Archaeological Study of Churches*, Council for British Archaeology, 1976.

PENOYRE, J. and J., *Houses in the Landscape. A Regional study of Vernacular Building Styles in England and Wales*, Faber, 1978.

Chapter 6. The PRO and other National Collections

Most of the institutions mentioned in this chapter distribute leaflets outlining their collections and the arrangements for readers. In addition, larger guides should be available in most public libraries:

Guide to the Contents of the Public Record Office, HMSO, 1963–68.

COX, J., and PADFIELD, T., *Tracing your Ancestors in the Public Record Office*, HMSO, 1981.

MORTON, A., and DONALDSON, G., *British National Archives and the Local Historian. A Guide to Official Record Publications*, Historical Association, 1980.

NICKSON, M. A. E., *The British Library. Guide to the Catalogues and Indexes of the Department of Manuscripts*, 1978.

WAGNER, A. R., *The Records and Collections of the College of Arms*, Burke's Peerage, 1974.

BOND, M. F., *Guide to the Records of Parliament*, HMSO, 1971.

On the sessional papers of the two houses of parliament, mentioned in connection with House of Lords Records office (p. 145), the introductory works include:

POWELL, W. R., *Local History from Blue Books: A Select List of the Sessional Papers of the House of Commons*, Historical Association, 1962.

FORD, P. and G., *Select List of British Parliamentary Papers, 1833–99*, revised edition, Shannon, Irish Universities Press, 1969.

FORD, P. and G., *Guide to Parliamentary Papers: what they are, how to find them, how to use them*, revised edition, Shannon, Irish Universities Press, 1972.

Chapter 7. Writing and Publication

Most of this chapter is based closely on my own experience in local history publishing and there is no full-scale guide to the subject. Three titles are worth mentioning, of which the first is the most useful:

DYMOND, D., *Writing Local History*, British Association for Local History, 1981.

HODGKISS, A. G., *Maps for Books and Theses*, Newton Abbot, David & Charles, 1970.

DYMOND, D., *Writing a Church Guide*, Church Information Office and British Association for Local History, 1977.

INDEX